Verbal & Non-Verbal Reality

*"When You Know What the Mind Is
You'll Know What is Not Real"*

mike marinelli

"Verbal and Non Verbal Reality"
Atlanta, Georgia 4/2024 Copyright by Mike Marinelli.
All rights reserved.
First Edition 2024

The United States of America copyright laws protect this book, prohibiting reproduction or use unless authorized by the author in writing.

Preface

In this book, I'll present what I consider a self-evident truth about how our language has conditioned the mind of almost everyone to fabricate a personality that includes one's identities, desires and preferences, attachments, and beliefs. These have created a mental and verbal environment manufactured in our imagination and minds. Word meanings can be configured conceptually to provide meaning to what comes and goes in our physical and cognitive experiences. It also provides meaning, value, and functionality through thought creation. Verbal thoughts created by word meanings can develop ideas and concepts that give a virtual mental reality experience. This language-based mental construct is what I call a Verbal Reality, which has been conditioned conceptually by shaping word meanings and concepts to fabricate a conceptual reality that may misrepresent reality "as it is."

There's a holistic and organic reality that is Non-Verbal. This reality is that of energy, consciousness, perception, and awareness, and is not a conceptual reality fabricated by language. It functions silently in space and time, and it is a reality that we all share. A nonverbal reality is the closest we can come to the center of our existence. The nonverbal aspect of this reality can be experienced by all through meditation, self-inquiry, and mindful practices. Universal and cosmic energies emerge from consciousness to create the conditions for our phenomenal existence in form, both physically and mentally. This aspect of existence is incomprehensible to the egoic mind. And because it is "beyond" conceptual comprehension, it is called the "Absolute." It is beyond all dualistic concepts of language.

In Part I, **Verbal Reality,** I'll reveal how verbal language shapes many aspects of our lives. Language forces the mind to bond with conceptual ideas and beliefs, and these attachments condition the mind to fabricate unconscious and habitual behavior. These conditioned patterns are imprinted in the mind and create one's reality to be either a positive or negative experience. It shapes how we view our existence conceptually.

Our languages create a verbal reality that has fabricated the human experience of subjective (internal) and objective (external) reality. As we delve into these discussions, it will become evident how language is a semantic matrix that can imagine and fabricate conceptual experiences of the past, present, and future.

Understanding that most people have been somewhat conditioned by the language they speak reveals how impactful language can be in shaping one's life experiences. Language creates a verbal environment that conceptualizes our experiences of reality, which is profound and phenomenal.

In Part II, **Non-Verbal Reality,** I'll explore the nonverbal aspects of how we experience an unconditioned reality without the use of language. Consciousness and awareness are the sources of energies, vibrations, and frequencies. These sources create the conditions for our physical and psychological existence as consciousness transforms into physical matter, mental states, and life experiences. We are naturally connected to numerous universal and cosmic processes that are inherently fundamental. These include earthly and cosmic energies such as the energetic fields of electricity, electromagnetism, light, sound, and the quantum field. These fundamental processes create the conditions that give rise to all relative phenomena.

From my point of view, we can experience the present moments of our life 'as it is' without being unconsciously attached to the constructs of conceptual fabrications. "Conceptual fabrication" means that everything and every experience has been conceptualized through language to derive its meaning and existential verity. It will become evident that the conceptualized mind is unsustainable as thoughts come and go, and everything is in flux of change.

With conceptual thinking, awareness is full of thoughts that come and go. Empty awareness is the key to knowing what the thinking mind is and how it renders reality for every person. The mind is fictitious; you'll see why I say that as we proceed.

Many obstacles prevent us from knowing who we are and what is real and unreal, and this will be explored from many perspectives. I intend that this discourse will have value in expanding the reader's awareness of what is not real about this life journey.

This book originated from the experiences and knowledge acquired over a sixty-year spiritual journey, which inspired me to share this knowledge. My meditations and contemplations revealed that language conceptualized my reality experience through conceptual thinking and that its unconscious use created a verbal and conditioned reality. The fabrication of a verbal construct of reality became evident, and it revealed what is untrue and irrelevant in my life's experiences. A conceptual experience of reality may not be authentic, and what appears and disappears in our awareness may not be perceived "as it is."

In my journey, I have delved deeply into the mechanics of the mind in so many ways that this exploration has revealed what the mind is and isn't. I recognized that I don't have to be identified, conditioned, or attached to anything physical or conceptual. I intend for anyone reading this to understand their true nature and the conceptual realities they create and experience. And especially how a verbal matrix unconsciously creates realities one may not want to experience. These insights are what I hope to share, and they may have some value for anyone who is on a similar life journey, committed to knowing what is real or not.

Disclaimer: *Albert Einstein is often credited with saying,* **"Problems cannot be solved with the same mindset that created them."** *This quote suggests that to solve a problem, one must approach it from a different perspective or mindset. Similarly, this book is created by language, a conditioned mindset similar to what could be stated as the problem, as quoted above. The very language used to create this book should be taken to point to a greater awareness and perspective to see all appearances of the present moment "as it is" and not to conceptualize it within a verbal context.*

Acknowledgments

I want to acknowledge those who gave me such good advice in writing this book. We're all on our journey, and I'd like to express my gratitude to those who provided their critique and consultation. Our discussions have been profoundly insightful and helpful in developing this content.

Dr. John Boli, Professor Emeritus, Sociology, Emory University, Atlanta, GA.

I'd like to thank Professor Boli for providing such valuable and honest critiques and contributing to the editing of this book. His critique was invaluable.

Mark Adams, Zen Buddhist Priest

For many years, our discussions have covered most of the topics in this book and contributed to its content. I'd like to thank Mark for his assistance with the editing and for providing his valuable insights.

Lester Herbertson, Design and Graphics Artist

Lester is a talented artist from Atlanta, GA, who created all of the graphics and illustrations for the book, including the cover. Our friendship and Shamanic connection developed over many years, and I'd like to thank him for his artistic abilities and patience in creating the graphics for this book.

Dr. Vern Morgan

For many years, Dr. Vern has been a spiritual brother. Our discussions have always been insightful. He contributed to the editing and provided his consultant advice, which helped present the book's content.

Alex Burch

My son-in-law, Alex, is an avid science fiction reader and has provided correlations between similar concepts in this book. Thank you, Alex, for helping to publish this book.

Tom Ballinger

Tom has been a good friend for many years. Our discussions have always been fruitful. Tom's view sometimes differs from mine, and his commentary on the book's content has challenged me. Thank you!

John Marinelli

My brother, John, is a Christian Poet and Writer who has published many books. John's expertise in publishing and editing has been insightful, and I appreciate his commentary, even though we "agree to disagree."

Michael Burk

Michael is a metaphysical poet and energy sound healer. Michael provided some beautiful poetry from his recent book Dancing with the Shadows. Poem: "Equanimy of Energies," Mountain Arbor Press, Georgia – Copyright 2023

Table of Contents

PART I

Verbal Reality: Introduction 3
Chapter 1 Verbal Reality 15
Chapter 2 Subjective and Objective Reality 45
Chapter 3 What is the Mind? 51
Chapter 4 Emotions and Feelings 87
Chapter 5 The Ego and Personality 97
Chapter 6 Verbal Language Creates Dualistic Thinking 115
Chapter 7 The Language of Mathematics 120
Chapter 8 Verbal Language as a Manipulation Tool 124
Chapter 10 Artificial Intelligence 137
Chapter 11 Conceptual Realization 147

PART II

Non-Verbal Reality: Introduction 155

Chapter 12 Energy, Vibration, and Frequency 160

Chapter 12 Non-Verbal Language in Art 171

Chapter 13 Eastern and Western Religions 175

Chapter 14 Metaphysics, Mysticism, and Spirituality 185

Chapter 15 Suspending Conceptual Thinking 193

Chapter 16 Consciousness and Awareness 197

Chapter 17 Mindfulness and Spiritual Awareness 213

Chapter 18 Spiritual Practices and Rituals 218

Chapter 19 What is Enlightenment and Self-Realization? 241

Chapter 20 Grace and Synchronicity 250

Chapter 21 Waking Up From the Dream 255

Chapter 22 Living in the Present Moment 258

Chapter 23	The Universal Mind and the Wisdom Mind	264
Chapter 24	Guru Nitya Chaitanya Yati	269
Conclusion		278
About the Author		281
Appendix I		283
Appendix II		286

VERBAL REALITY

PART ONE

Verbal Reality

Introduction

We'll begin by exploring how language impacts our experience of reality. Language occupies a large amount of our intellectual energy and provides us with a tool to communicate, share ideas, and create abstract concepts. Humans have used language throughout history to develop ideologies, religions, and personal identities. We label everything in the physical and mental universe with word meanings that have conceptualized our experiences through a language matrix. Even a person's identity is defined by language to create a persona made up in one's mind. Knowing how the ego interacts with a conceptual fabrication of what one thinks is reality is essential.

Our language defines and conditions how we think and observe our present-moment experiences. We live in a matrix of imagined and fabricated thoughts that produce a conceptualized experience of much of our reality. We perceive the world internally and externally with our five senses and by what the mind cognizes. The appearance and disappearance of objects in our awareness come and go constantly. Everything is continually changing and in motion. When defined by words or thoughts, these appearances provide an existential condition and a value structure that gives our perceptions meaning, purpose, and functionality. However, this is experienced within a fabricated conceptual context. This is how we differentiate ourselves from the animal kingdom. We are "language thinking" human beings that communicate with each other as such. We have verbalized and conceptualized most of our experience of reality.

A language matrix filters our experience of what appears and disappears in our senses and minds. A conceptual understanding of reality may conceal the authenticity of what is actually occurring and appearing in space and time. Each person has a language matrix uniquely tailored and conditioned by their life experiences. To understand what is real or not, we must gain insight into the nature of our reality, subjectively, objectively, and beyond the confines of language. We should also consider what exists as a nonverbal reality in our experience of the present moment, which is changing continuously.

In one's mind, a conceptualization of reality can take shape in many forms and experiences. Here's an example: in a person's mind, they may have created an entire mental environment around their occupation. Many of us may have identified ourselves with our occupation and job title. After many years on the job, an occupational ego has constructed an entire work environment in one's mind. This is a conceptualization of what is experienced in the mind that creates the mind's view of this occupational reality. A person's lifestyle and behavior conform to their beliefs and identities within their occupational environment and its relationships. In that person's mind, they have an occupational personality and an identity within the workplace for their various occupational roles. Like an actor, when the worker goes home, he may change clothes, shower, and shake off the occupational role he just left. We play this game unconsciously without being aware that it is conceptually fabricated in our minds. When we shed all the games, roles, attachments, preferences, and identities of ourselves, we can be our authentic naked selves unfabricated and still be able to function in our occupational roles genuinely and spontaneously.

While engaged in various occupational "day gigs," I always saw myself first as a musician who was committed to a lifelong spiritual journey. These identities detached me from identifying myself with any job, allowing me to function in many roles without getting attached to them personally. I was always aware that I was performing the activities of a job that was always grounded in the present moment which enabled me to fulfill that job's requirements to the best of my ability, unattached to any results or outcomes.

Thus, we should explore and differentiate our authentic reality, i.e., seeing all that appears "as it is," from a verbal reality, i.e., conceptualizing it. Conceptual reality is a verbal commentary or story fabricated by what one believes, values, and is attached to. This will become clear as we continue.

I don't want to give the impression that I'm against all linguistic conditioning (verbal conditioning) or that it is terrible for the human race. Language is necessary and natural for everyone to navigate their reality functionally, safely, and purposefully. Language used in society allows everyone to participate and be engaged with one another through communication and conceptual interaction. This is necessary to create societal growth, stability, camaraderie, and transactional interaction with the world we live in.

Awareness is critical to gaining insight and understanding of what presents itself in every present-moment experience. We should initially abide in our awareness as silent witnesses who observe all appearances without conceptualization. Meditation provides an awareness that is a silent witness in this context. This would be the first step to awakening to what is true about ourselves and the world.

What is Reality?

I see a "Relative" reality in space and time and an "Absolute" reality beyond space and time. Reality can be experienced in both ways.

- "Relative Reality" is the life experience of existing in a conceptualized and filtered reality using language to create an abstract understanding of what appears in our minds and perceptions. It is a language-based grid that allows the collective population to communicate information and interact with all environments, physically and intellectually.

- Absolute Reality is beyond what is relative in space and time and is beyond dualistic thinking, i.e., good/bad, happy/sad, etc. Absolute, in this sense, is not a transcendental or transactional experience; it is neither this nor that and not dualistic. Nor is it a subject or an object, and it is beyond the mind's comprehension. It cannot be experienced as a conceptual reality. The "Absolute" is the ground of existence that manifests from consciousness, the primordial field (possibly quantum) that forms all existence. Consciousness takes forms similar to how waves form based on the conditions of the ocean.

- Absolute is beyond existence and non-existence, truth or untruth, life or death, nirvana (a state of self-realization), or samsara (an illusive state), as these are merely conceptual manifestations of the conditioned egoic mind. Because it is "beyond," it is not a concept the mind can comprehend.

- The Absolute cannot be defined conceptually using words and language. This primordial and cohesive fabric of consciousness takes forms that appear as the phenomenal Universe. Is it a simulation? An illusion? Does the reality that we perceive have any existential substance?

What is Defined as Reality?

This is a profound question that philosophers and scientists have pondered for centuries. There's no single, universally accepted answer, as reality depends on many factors, especially in the context of relative truth.

Some of these factors include:

- Perspective: Our individual experiences, beliefs, and senses shape our perception of reality. What feels real to me might not be the same for someone else.

- Science: Studies in physics, neuroscience, and other fields give us insights into the objective features of our universe, like matter, energy, and natural laws. But they don't answer the existential question about "being."

- Philosophy: Different philosophical schools offer diverse perspectives on reality. Some emphasize objective truths, while others explore subjective interpretations and the limits of human knowledge.

Here are some different ways to think about relative reality:

- The physical world encompasses everything we can observe and measure, from atoms to galaxies. Science describes this reality with increasing accuracy but can't necessarily explain its ultimate nature.

- The subjective experience: Each individual perceives the world through their unique and personal conditioning and mindset, influenced by memories, emotions, and beliefs. This personal reality exists alongside the objective one.

- The objective experience: Objective reality typically refers to things existing independently of individual perception or interpretation. It's assumed to be a fixed, universal truth about the world, like the laws of physics, even if no one observes them.

- The social construction: Shared ideas, language, and cultural norms contribute to our understanding of reality. What seems natural in one society might be deemed different in another.

Why Should It Matter if We Experience Reality Verbally or Non-verbally?

The advantage of "seeing" what is appearing and disappearing to our senses with an empty mind is that we can subjectively and objectively observe what is occurring in the present moment without conceptualizing it. Then, it is experienced as it is nonverbally. With no conceptualization, we see all "as it is" authentically. Seeing clearly "what is" enables us to make the right choices to engage or participate (or not) as it is occurring in the present moment. In other words, we aren't reacting automatically to subconscious conditioning, which automatically and unconsciously causes 95% of our behavior. When you only see one way to respond to a situation, it may be a conditioned response; you may not see any other possibilities. This will be discussed in detail further in this discourse.

The Matrix is a 1999 science fiction movie that depicts a dystopian future in which humanity is unknowingly trapped inside a simulated reality in which intelligent machines have been created to distract humans from seeing what is real.

Much like the movie The Matrix, we live in a conceptualized reality that artificially represents the life we perceive through the mind's conceptual thinking. Most of us live in a dreamlike state where conceptualized mirages of thoughts persist and appear and disappear continuously in our minds. The process of waking up from this conditioned state is to gain clarity and visibility in seeing how verbal and nonverbal language is an interplay of consciousness expressing itself by a mind's view.

Discovering what is true about our lives is a journey of self-discovery and enlightenment. If one is committed to this journey, it is evident that one must come to understand that language and conceptual thinking are simply a skill set like so many other skill sets that one has acquired. Humans use conceptual thinking to navigate their life's experience functionally, so much of what we think and say is irrelevant to what we are experiencing. Language and conceptual thinking should be stored in a mental toolbox to respond to appearances in our awareness, subjectively and objectively, whenever needed.

Chapter 1

Verbal Reality

The mind's internal processing creates, records, and stores our perceptions and observations of present-moment experiences. It creates conceptualized content by judging, analyzing, and categorizing subjects and objects that appear and disappear in the mind through language and thought content. This is primarily accomplished using language to create a verbal and conceptual reality. This mental reality is fed by the appearance of thought patterns and mental imagery that gets processed and transformed into conceptual experiences through language, all of which happens in the mind and what I call a "Verbal Reality." This is presumed to be experienced in the mind as if it is one's reality. In my experience, I didn't find this to be true.

We have verbalized and conceptualized our entire experience of reality. For example:

- Everything has a name and a form, defined by a vocabulary of word meanings.

- Word meanings imprint thoughts and concepts in our minds, creating our identities, attachments, desires, and beliefs.

- We are taught to think using our language to communicate and be creative and spontaneous in context with verbal conceptualization.

- Language is a matrix of conceptualized abstractions that can filter our perceptions of reality negatively or positively.

- An abstract matrix of language and the experience of conceptual thinking do not provide the correct understanding of reality "as it is." Reality is viewed through a conceptual thinking process that proliferates abstractions that filter our experiences of what is perceived as reality.

- Conceptual realities are not fundamental, as they are purely conceptual and phenomenal.

- In a relative sense, conceptual realities experienced by most people have a valid existence within their context. Suppose a person is unaware of any other reality except how they have conceptualized it. In that case, a conceptualized reality is authentic to the person who thinks and believes it's real in every aspect, even though the mind fabricates its appearances conceptually.

The programmed content in the mind is based on conceptual thoughts, ideas, imaginations, memories, beliefs, attachments, preferences, etc., and these appearances have no substantial existence inherent in themselves. Once appearances are formulated in the mind and provided with a conceptualized existence, they become artificial, virtual, and abstract. They create a conceptual existence, manifesting appearances of physical and mental forms that are empty of any reality substance. And this can be verified by science-related fields such as neuroscience and psychology. What appears in our senses is perceived and processed conceptually within a preconditioned environment where appearances have existential verity only in their fabricated state. The egoic mind is a mental construct of name, form, and a value system providing a substantial virtual environment in which to engage and participate.

Verbal language has similarities to computer software. Language is like a mental operating system that has been incrementally programmed in the mind through many years of experiential and educational conditioning. This "conditioning" or "programming" of the mind may be similar to computer programming. This is not to say that the conceptualized mind is the same as a computer's processor.

In a purely conceptual context, the mind can be programmed or trained to think, believe, and interact with subjective and objective realities in a mostly fabricated reality experience built on imagination and belief systems. Language and conceptual thinking are networked into our biological and mental infrastructures that interact with our five senses and perceptual faculties in the brain. Our brain is an interface that connects us to what we call our mind, and the mind is a construct of consciousness that connects us to a collective mind that provides the societal structures that enable communication and intellectual interaction required for functionality and participation.

As the brain receives and transmits mental and physical information like thoughts, emotions, feelings, desires, attachments, preferences, and beliefs, it transforms them into a conceptual matrix created by verbal language. This conceptual matrix can imagine and fabricate present-moment experiences that may not be authentic. Most people that I know conceptualize their reality.

What is Meant by Fabricating Realities, and What are Conceptual Realities?

By fabricating realities, we may misinterpret, rationalize, or make conclusions about what we have experienced purely through our conceptualization process, a construct of language and thought content. These concepts impact our behavior. We become attached to these concepts of what we "think" exists and what we "believe" we are experiencing as being true; it may not be so once the mind stops conceptualizing reality and sees everything "as it is" without using a language-based context.

Without living in your mind as thoughts about everything, you perceive a reality of actual appearances "as they are" and not conceptually what you may have imagined or viewed them to be. This is impossible if the mind conceptualizes and defines every experience through language and symbols. To see reality "as it is," the mind must be empty of thought conceptualization. This is not a transcendental experience. It's just seeing everything without "thinking" about what it is. This is a more authentic way of seeing and experiencing one's present-moment reality.

Conceptual reality may be viewed like this: If you have strong political or religious views, they have been conditioned or programmed in your mind. When you discuss these topics, you speak from a highly opinionated and rationalized view to make your point and accommodate your beliefs and preferences. All political or religious views are conceptual. They require a thought process that uses language and conceptual thinking to derive some understanding or conclusion that forms or suits one's beliefs. These concepts and thoughts are fabrications of political or religious ideologies that people identify with and they cause biases. Are they real?

There are no religious or political views or ideologies when all conceptual thinking is suspended. They are dependent upon language and conceptual thought for their existence. When you are political or religious, you engage in these topics as if they are real. Are they? They are when you are conceptually identified with a point of view. They are genuine to a person if that's the only way they can see things, and they have no other awareness of something that is otherwise. Also, if people are conditioned so that they hold on to their point of view and will not accept any others, there's almost a total disconnect, ignoring any possibility of an authentic or positive relationship. When conceptual thinking is suspended, one settles into one's understanding of being silently aware and in harmony with the present moment experience, unfabricated.

It is essential to know what is unreal or irrelevant. Engaging in a political or religious discussion may be relevant if the situation is conducive to a civil interaction and both parties are willing to create a positive outcome. It's a choice! If you are aware of the present moment without conceptualizing it, you can make an appropriate choice to become engaged in whatever appears as your reality or not. This is freedom!

To understand reality "as it is," the mind has to be awake, alert, and attentive to the present moment and in a state of clarity as subjects and objects appear and disappear in our senses and minds. When the mind is empty, still, and silent, without words or conceptual thoughts, the present moment is viewed "as it is." It is not conceptualized by language. When mental activity is reduced to a more primal condition, no subjects and objects appear as conceptual thoughts. When all thoughts are subsided, reality is seen precisely "as it is" without verbal commentary. When no subjects and objects appear in the mind conceptually, only one thing exists: the "now" experience of pure consciousness unfiltered or colored in any way, shape, or form. Conscious awareness is the cohesive factor that unifies and connects all creations emerging from one consciousness, as the many aspects we experience and differentiate.

Another example: The ocean is a body of water that forms waves due to conditions. Similarly, consciousness is the all-pervasive creative energy that takes form like waves in the sea. The waves cannot be separated from the ocean. Likewise, physical and mental forms are the appearances and expressions of consciousness, and the appearance of forms cannot be separated from consciousness, either.

Becoming aware of what you have conceptualized as your reality is crucial because you can become attached to a mentally constructed way of seeing your experiences or feelings about everything. This conceptualization may condition and wire your brain to perceive and conceive of everything through an imagined existence that may not be authentic and lack substantial validity. A conceptualized reality can also be damaging and cause suffering, either mentally or physically, if the conceptual content is destructive or harmful and manifests negatively.

The advantage of abiding in a state of empty awareness, without conceptual thinking, is that it is the most harmonious state one can experience. It is a unifying experience that reveals our genuine connection to the Universe. This state is not fabricated or contaminated by conceptual thought.

Most people think that a conceptualized reality is our default state. Is it? Or is it a fabricated conceptualization superimposed on the present moment to create an intellectual experience in the individual and collective mind? A more accurate and authentic view is when empty awareness is experienced as unconditioned consciousness, where all is experienced without identification or conceptualization.

Undefined and unconditioned reality is an empirical experience of awareness that sees what appears as it is. I think it's okay to conceptualize and even fabricate realities if it is not an unconscious behavior. With full awareness, there is always a choice to see clearly (or not) all that appears in your mind as your reality experience.

Advantages of Language

Language is a complex and fascinating system that allows us to communicate, express ourselves, and share our thoughts and ideas with others. It should be used as a tool, like any other tool. The problem is that language has been given the authority as the predominant means for understanding and valuing our experiences. Language provides informational and intellectual knowledge of the present moment within the context of a conceptual reality. It is unconsciously functioning as the norm of our intellectually conceived experiences.

Language is essential to the Human race. It's not just about words; it's a system of symbols, rules, and patterns we use to create meaning. Language has a structure comprising building blocks like sounds, phrases, and sentences. Words and symbols have specific meanings that we understand and agree upon. These elements are combined according to grammatical rules to form meaningful expressions that develop into ideas, concepts, and beliefs. Language is all about conveying meaning. We also use language to express more abstract concepts of feelings and emotions.

There's nothing wrong with using language to function and express ourselves. What is detrimental to one's life experience is to live in a virtual reality and not know that you are living in one. This can cause suffering, pain, and a negative experience, which can be fabricated by how one thinks and what one believes. Becoming free of this is an enlightening and joyful experience that reveals itself once the shackles of conceptual thinking are seen through and awareness expands to provide a clear view of what appears as your reality in the present moment.

The primary function of language is communication. We use language to share information, ideas, and feelings. It allows us to build relationships, collaborate, and learn from each other. Language is also a powerful tool for creativity. We can use it to create stories, poems, songs, and other art forms. Language allows us to imagine new worlds and possibilities. It has immense power that influences every part of our life. Thousands of languages are spoken worldwide, each with its unique characteristics. This diversity reflects the different cultures and histories of human societies.

Linguistics is the study of language, a vast and fascinating field. Linguists explore the various aspects of language, from its structure and meaning to its history and evolution.

Here are some additional thoughts on language:

- Language is constantly evolving. New words are continuously created, and old words can have new meanings.

- Language is not just about spoken words. It can also be expressed through writing, sign language, and art.

- Language is a powerful tool that can be used for good or bad. It's essential to be aware of language's power and use it responsibly.

Language is a relative and finite aspect of the human experience that works within space and time. It enables the creation of thoughts, ideas, concepts, beliefs, judgments, and preferences. As mentioned, the mind carries it around like a mental toolbox of conceptually conceived ideas and thoughts.

Our spoken language defines and categorizes all that appears in the physical universe. It is an interface of mental processing that conceptually describes our experiences of the past, present, and future. However, as we shall see, a limited view can narrow our perceptions and experiences of reality.

Understanding how language affects our desires, attachments, beliefs, and the creative aspects of being human is essential to connect and live in harmony with everything. We use language to understand and communicate our experiences to ourselves and each other. It provides an abstract understanding of our mental and physical experiences. This understanding empowers us to be aware of the present moment through a wisdom mind that is always connected universally and collectively.

Physical and Mental Components of Language Processing

Language is like a bio-interface, a system that processes information between the brain and the conscious and subconscious mind. Language provides pathways of information that get wired into the subconscious mind to enable a neural network of preconceived and automatic reactionary patterns that are resourceful and necessary to navigate all dimensions of a person's reality experience. The subconscious mind is a vast database of information, impressions, and conditioned patterns of behavioral operations that work behind the scenes to provide substance and function to our present-moment experiences. It automates our responses to provide conditioned reactions to one's reality. It contains predetermined and reactionary programs wired in the brain that are integrated into the conceptual mind for functional and survival purposes. The subconscious mind sits below the conscious mind and is hidden from conscious view.

Like many word processing applications, the mind, through language, provides us with a "mental language processor" that can conceptually process language information. In the same way, a person uses a word processor to express information and meaningful ideas, such as writing a book. A word processor is a tool that uses language to communicate meaning and value in creating ideas, concepts, beliefs, etc., through the construct of language.

The brain and body are the biological hardware of our physical existence. Verbal language creates our conceptual existence and acts as a filter to conceptualize our experiences.

Verbal conceptualization is conditioned in the mind to enable a comprehensive mental environment for navigating the human experience by exploring, defining, and understanding all appearances and disappearances of the present moment that come and go in one's awareness. However, awareness is always in a pure state of emptiness devoid of conceptual content. It is like a movie screen on which all images are projected—a blank screen.

When you hear someone speak, the language program in your brain listens to the sounds and tries to figure out what they mean. It also helps you form sounds and words when you speak. The brain comprises billions of tiny parts that create sounds, words, phrases, and sentences. It's like a puzzle with many pieces that fit together just right. It provides a vocabulary of word meanings organized to render our psycho-physical experiences abstract. This happens through mental processing, creating a simulated or virtual experience of our perceptions and cognitive activity. Its program is impressive because it lets us learn new things, share our ideas, and connect with others. It also allows us to create stories, poems, and songs. It's like a virtual game!

The Human Brain

The biological brain is similar to the hard drive in a computer. It is a bio-interface formatted to enable physical and mental processing. It is like a radio transmitter or receiver. It receives and transmits information abstractly to the body and mind.

Additionally, the information processing that the brain transmits and receives can create a conceptually conceived mind that appears to form subjective and objective experiences from abstract confections of memories from the past and speculative expectations of the future. In the same way, you observe objects in the outside world, you can also experience mental objects or activities in your mind. The observer of the mind, body, and outside world is the energy field we call awareness. This awareness observes everything that is projected onto it. As mentioned, it is like a blank screen with projected images appearing and disappearing. The brain and the mind process information within the energy field of awareness, which is always an observation. The observer and the object being observed are experienced as one when there are no conceptualizations.

Conditioning the Mind with a Language Program

A digital language program for computer programming uses computer language or "code" to create specific instructions (algorithms) and electronic neural networks. Many computer languages, such as Python, C++, and Java, are used to program a computer. These computer languages create specific instructions and computations that enable the computer to function to carry out various tasks and provide specific outcomes. These instructions are called Algorithms or particular commands that provide the computer with instructions to accomplish these tasks or outcomes.

The human experience of verbal conditioning is much more vast than any computer can come close to, even though computers can compute and analyze information much faster than humans. However, the analogy is appropriate, considering that a functional mind engaged in human activity is a conceptually conceived apparatus conditioned to behave in specific ways when stimulated by human interaction or environmental factors. This doesn't mean that our mind is a computerized machine. It is much more than that. For instance, what is the smell of a rose? What is the taste of ice cream? These experiences can be described verbally by language but can never provide a person with the experience of smelling a rose or tasting ice cream. Language and conceptual knowledge can never offer a physical sensory experience.

There's an underlying, pervasive awareness that is cognitive and perceives reality "as it is" when conceptual thinking has subsided. I see this as the default state of consciousness always present whether or not conceptual thinking has been suspended.

The verbal use of words and word meanings are symbols. These symbols can condition the mind to conceive and perceive the world and all objects within it as a conceptual experience created in the mind. Memories of conceptual experiences of reality become the mind's contents, giving it a dynamic and energetic existence. These experiences are mentally experienced when the mind is conditioned and attached to a verbal language for conceptually expressing and experiencing the present moment.

Our language has characteristics similar to those of a computer operating system. It is programmed with algorithms and values that provide definition and meaning as the present moment appears and disappears in our awareness. This symbolic system creates possibilities for understanding our experiences, memories, and thoughts within a mental context of conceptual ideas and values. In a sense, it creates an imagined experience that impacts how we understand ourselves and our world. The symbols and rules of verbal language can be organized into logical structures to develop ideas, concepts, and beliefs, enabling us to imagine and experience a conceptualized virtual reality. It is truly phenomenal.

Language is used by cultures and societies to create a shared reality. But it can also be used to deceive and manipulate people. However, it is essential to remember that language is similar to computer software and application systems. It's an interface to define and understand the physical world through abstract thought and how we experience space and time, i.e., the past, present, and an imagined future. It is not always accurate and is always a limited or individualized view conditioned by the person experiencing it. There are as many conceptual realities as there are people, each with their own.

The conditioning aspect of language began the moment we were born and was mostly done without our conscious awareness or consent. At this early age, when we were receptive to whatever symbol systems we were exposed to, our minds were conditioned to perceive and interpret the experience of the present moment in a defined and limited way.

What is Conceptual Thinking?

A concept is an abstract idea or general notion representing a category or class of objects, events, or experiences. It is a mental construct that helps us understand and organize the world that we experience. Concepts can represent physical objects, such as a "dog" or a "tree," or they can convey more abstract ideas, such as "justice" or "freedom." They play a crucial role in cognition, language, and communication, allowing us to categorize, classify, and make sense of the vast information we encounter.

If I have a preconceived thought or idea that I'm going to go to a party and have fun, this concept will set the stage for the experience to come to fruition. On the other hand, if I had an idea that the party would be boring and not fun, I would have this expectation and probably experience this in reality. All of this is mental! It's a conceptual fabrication that exists in the present moment in our minds. Still, it doesn't have substantial reality in the present moment because these are purely "thoughts" about what is appearing and disappearing in our minds. Don't get me wrong; the authentic reality beyond conceptual thinking does exist and can be perceived by our senses and the mind. Its appearance in our awareness is present, but it doesn't appear with a built-in verbal commentary unless the mind has been conditioned to view everything conceptually.

Conceptual thought is a mental activity that creates understanding and reasoning about abstract ideas intellectually. Conceptual means that it is a fabricated construct of thoughts, ideas, and understandings, all designed by the language used to explain, define, and provide an intellectual experience of the now-moments of our lives. It involves identifying patterns, connecting seemingly disparate ideas, and forming generalizations. Conceptual thinking is essential for various cognitive tasks, including problem-solving, creativity, and decision-making.

Conceptual thinking is a cognitive process that involves going beyond the surface level of information to understand underlying principles and relationships. It involves:

- Identifying and manipulating abstract ideas and concepts.
- It lets us recognize patterns and similarities across different situations and draw conclusions.

- It provides critical thinking ability for analyzing and evaluating information to reach informed conclusions.

- Its creative aspect enables us to generate new ideas and solutions by combining existing concepts with new ways of thinking.

The Relationship Between Thought and Language

Language is a powerful tool that shapes and influences our thoughts. We use words to represent concepts, ideas, and experiences. Here's how they are connected:

- Language helps us form thoughts. Learning new words allows us to think about new concepts more clearly.

- Language helps us organize thoughts. It allows us to categorize information, make connections between ideas, and build complex arguments.

- Language helps us communicate thoughts. Language is the primary way we share our thoughts and ideas with others.

The most crucial aspect of conceptual thinking is that it plays a critical role in shaping our behavior positively or negatively. It influences how we perceive the world, make decisions, and interact with others.

Conceptual thinking is a powerful tool for navigating the complexities of life. It allows us to understand others' perspectives, empathize with their feelings, and build meaningful relationships. We can interpret social cues, understand nonverbal communication, and communicate our thoughts and ideas effectively.

However, conceptual thinking creates a mental environment superimposed on the now-moment. It establishes and filters our realities and keeps us confined within a mental state limited by how it is conditioned or programmed.

Overall, mental activity, including conceptual thinking, limits our worldview regarding reality. Conceptual thinking conceives a worldview that becomes limited to a fabricated experience. We live out our lives in a conditioned state of limitations imposed on us by the very language we use.

Conceptualizing the experience of the present moment as a reality may conceal authentic reality 'as it is.' In other words, the authenticity of reality without conceptual thinking is always present, and it is just what it is; it doesn't require verbal definition unless it is needed for functionality within this conceptual view, which is perfectly appropriate in this context.

Even though language is a powerful tool for thought, it's important to remember that a whole world of thinking happens beyond words. This will be discussed in detail in Part II, "Non-Verbal Reality."

A Conceptual Matrix of Language and Thought

We experience most of our reality within a conceptually conditioned mind, creating a matrix of thought behavior we often abide by. In some ways, it has trapped us inside the mind, much like the movie "The Matrix." The matrix we live in is a language-based conceptualized reality, and most of us live in this matrix most of our lives. It conceptualizes our experiences by defining, categorizing, and interpreting the activities of our daily lives within the constructs of a mental environment that is all made up in our minds. A conceptual matrix is a world experienced in the mind and resides in mental concepts created by language.

This matrix of conceptualized reality is developed through educational, cultural, and individual experiences that have been conditioned and stored in the subconscious mind. This conditioning produces a representation of reality that continually creates cultures, societies, and institutions that depend totally on its symbolic and creative evolution.

It does have limitations, though:

- Language inherently simplifies and categorizes things. Real-world experiences are often nuanced, complex, and full of subtle variations that words might not capture. For example, the "redness" of a sunset is a single word representing a whole spectrum of light and color perception. This can lead to a sense of detachment from the richness of the lived experience.

- Language is a secondary representation system, coming after our direct, sensory experience of the world. When we translate an experience into words, it's already filtered through our cognitive processes and shaped by our vocabulary and understanding. This can lead to a feeling of distance from reality's immediate, raw sensory qualities.

- Our individual experiences and perspectives shape language. Words carry connotations and associations that vary from person to person, resulting in different interpretations of the same experience. This inherent subjectivity can limit our ability to understand and appreciate another person's reality fully.

- Certain aspects of reality simply cannot be translated into words. Emotions, spiritual experiences, and the ineffable qualities of nature can be difficult, if not impossible, to fully express through language. This can leave us feeling like there's more to reality than we can ever articulate.

- Language can be misused to frame experiences in a biased or misleading way. Language can distort or obscure reality through propaganda, misinformation, manipulation, gaslighting, and misunderstanding. This highlights the importance of being critical of language and recognizing its limitations in representing the truth.

Despite these limitations, language remains essential for navigating and understanding our environments and the world we experience. By acknowledging its limitations and using it carefully, we can still enjoy its immense power to connect with others, share experiences, and expand our understanding of reality. Exploring other forms of expression, such as art, music, and movement, can help us bridge the gap between language's limitations and the richness of lived experiences.

Language should be used as a tool, and one should know and be aware of its use and consequences. It's like having a toolbox of tools you can use at any time, knowing that language is an abstract representation of how we perceive reality. Although, beware! One could mistakenly use it to unconsciously identify with a conceptual reality devoid of awareness of what is being experienced in the present moment.

The perpetual streaming of conscious awareness transforms into an abstract experience of information and knowledge through our language. Language is only one medium of interacting with subjective and objective reality. In my experience, the ramifications of programming or conditioning the mind by conceptual thought have undermined one's default state of being, which I don't believe is conceptual. However, in a relative and dualistic sense, conceptual thought will feel normal if that's the only reference one can experience. A natural and unconditioned state of awareness will become evident as we proceed.

Experiencing reality through language is analogous to wearing a virtual headset that produces a multitude of virtual worlds or simulations of experiences. A linguistic headset is a virtualization that fabricates realities through the creativity of verbal and conceptual thought. It is a virtual experience that has no substantial existence. What appears and disappears in our headsets are conceptual appearances and experiences that are virtual phenomena. This virtualized experience is seen through a language-based mental process that is taken for granted and unconsciously appears natural.

I found that thoughts, concepts, images, or forms do not appear in a silent meditative state. The mind is one-pointed and focused on what occurs in awareness within a silent mind. Whatever appears is not grasped or causes entanglements. Thoughts are like passing clouds in the sky. When they are seen as irrelevant or ignored, they subside effortlessly.

Our perceptive faculties are limited regarding what they can experience and the content they can perceive. In other words, there may be sensory information that we cannot experience due to the limitations of the perceptual headset that we are looking through. As an American Cognitive

Psychologist, Donald Hoffman states, "We may have a cheap headset." Our sense perceptions don't see all possible perceptions because of the limitations of our perceptual apparatus. For example, more colors may exist in our color spectrum that we can't perceive due to the restrictions of our headsets. Could you imagine a color that exists, but you cannot perceive it? We have scientific devices that can enable us to perceive the subtle environments of the microscopic and atomic worlds, such as microscopes, etc.; these devices have provided views of existence that we would not otherwise perceive. Even the range of colors from ultraviolet to infrared light would be impossible without these devices, which extend our perceptive capacities.

Chapter 2: Subjective & Objective Reality

Chapter 2

Subjective and Objective Reality

Subjective Reality

In my experience, the conscious mind (the awake state) can be turned inward or outward. When turned inward, a subjective reality can be experienced either as empty awareness (no thoughts or images) or as a mental environment where cognition and perception are experienced as a conceptual experience created by language, thoughts, and imagination.

What appears in my mind is processed by the language I use for thought creation. And this is what creates my conceptual experience, designed by words and thoughts as they appear in my mind's internal awareness. This is what I call "subjective reality."

The conscious mind that is awake and aware also experiences feelings and emotions in the experience of the present moment. These emerge from mental or physical sensations in the body and mind that have a similar recurrence from the past, like a headache that may have been experienced multiple times in the past. Because this experience has occurred many times previously, it has been conceptualized into thoughts associated with them. For instance, a feeling or emotion may arise when it is noticed as a painful experience. The mind will draw its analysis of the experiences from the past that are similar and conceptualize the experience into a verbal context that is described as feelings or sensations. This is another internal process of the mind that experiences a subjective reality.

It's important to note that other internal senses are also crucial for our cognition and perception, such as:

- Proprioception: the sense of body awareness and position in space.
- Balance: the sense of equilibrium and spatial orientation.
- Thermoception: the sense of temperature.

Objective Reality

Objective reality exists outside the body and mind and is observed as an external experience as it appears and disappears in awareness. This reality seems separate from the internal mind and is experienced as "out there" or something "other."

It is presumed that the world of appearances, outside the body/mind, always exists even if no one can perceive them. The world is thought to exist independently of any individual mind or consciousness. In other words, the existential experience of the individual mind or consciousness is only possible by a living being.

Objective reality is ultimately experienced as physical appearances, independent of subjective interpretations or biases. Even the body is an external object that the mind can observe. It belongs to the physical existence of nature and worldly objects.

One of the primary considerations in understanding objective reality is that some aspects of reality, like language, morality, and social norms, are constructed and negotiated by human societies. Understanding the different interpretations and acknowledging their complexities is crucial for engaging in meaningful discussions about the nature of reality, knowledge, and our place in the world and universe.

Subjective and objective realities are dualistic experiences: a subjective and objective existence always plays out our lives in space and time within a conceptual context.

Subjective and Objective Perception

All subjects and objects, both physical and mental, become known when we observe them as they appear. If a tree falls in the forest, did it fall if there was no one there to observe it falling? If a thought appears in your mind, did it appear by itself, and who was there to observe it? We can also learn about subjects and objects through indirect knowledge utilizing descriptive and imaginary thinking processes.

Our conscious attention is like a spotlight that illuminates subjects and objects, whether we observe them mentally or physically. This light (awareness function) also illuminates thoughts appearing in the mind. This, along with their constant reappearances, provides the continuity for sustaining their presumptive existence, even though someone was not physically or mentally present to observe them.

Subjective Perception: Our mental perceptions are personal due to conditioning and entanglement that may have resulted in acquiring attachments or beliefs. Subjective perception is a cognitive experience when the mind's awareness perceives internal objects such as thoughts, opinions, emotions, or feelings appearing in the mind or as bodily sensations. A value is assigned to these perceptions that give them relevancy, influencing our behavior. This mental activity is observed and experienced when the mind's attention is turned within and not towards the outside world. When these appear in the mind's awareness, they are perceived internally.

Internal perception is experienced differently than the actual reality we are in. It is a mental experience of abstract appearances perceived by the mind. Our cognitive awareness assumes they are real just by their appearance. Mentally perceived thoughts don't have any actual substantial existence except in a conceptual sense fabricated by the mind.

Objective Perception: Objective perception is perceived outside the mind in one's physical environment. The physical body is also an object of the objective environment. It is assumed that these perceptions are real and that the perceived objects evolve and change over time.

Interestingly, when we observe a tree, it only comes into existence when our attention is focused on it, and only then is it perceived. When we turn our attention to some other object, the tree vanishes from our mind. Our mind remembers the tree within a mental space and time that provides and sustains its assumed continuity of existence even though it is just a memory. As mentioned, it is believed that objects exist whether observed or not. When the same objects are perceived repeatedly, it will be the same tree previously perceived even though it has entirely changed. Objective reality is the projections of our mind that are predictive experiences always assumed, whether observed or not. Consciousness seamlessly streams subjective and objective realities as they are repeatedly observed and perceived.

Chapter 3: What is the Mind?

Chapter 3

What is the Mind?

The Human Mind

The human mind may be categorized into the individual and the collective. The individual or personal mind is created through empirical and educational conditioning stored in the subconscious mind. Its conditioning is due to a language-based model learned throughout one's life, manifested by a fabricated frame of reference conceived conceptually through language. The individual mind comprises conceptual thought content that can create abstract conceptual experiences from language. It uses memories stored in the subconscious mind, and one's creative imagination to fabricate a conceptual reality to make sense (conceptually) of what appears and disappears in the present moment.

The collective mind is a mental space or field of creative energy formed from consciousness outside the body. It may be called the "collective mind" or possibly that which Carl Jung refers to as the "collective unconscious." This may also be referred to as the "Universal Mind." All individual minds are connected to the collective mind and have varying degrees of access to its thought content, which explains how many areas of new knowledge or science simultaneously emerge in parts of the world at the same time.

The mind is a construct of conceptual fabrications that take the form of thoughts, images, sensory impressions, and even emotions. Without these characteristics, the mind wouldn't exist, i.e., no thoughts - no mind.

The mind is neurologically wired to the brain, like a receiver and transmitter. It receives mental activity as thoughts, ideas, or concepts derived from the content of the individual or collective mind. These are transmitted through neural networks to assimilate and communicate via thinking, speech, or writing. The mind processes conceptual information based on what is stored in the collective and subconscious mind, primarily verbally constructed concepts conceived by language.

Each person has a connection to and varying access to the mental content of the individual and collective mind. This intuitive connection emerges through the conditioned and unconditioned aspects of the person's psyche. Both the individual and collective mind influence the personality (ego), much like accessing the many aspects of the quantum field where all versions and possibilities of creation exist.

Thought structures of language content create and sustain a verbal reality, thus creating a mind that functions conceptually. Without such, the mind doesn't exist as we know it. I see the mind exists when thoughts, ideas, or concepts appear in one's awareness. The mind that most people associate with doesn't exist without conceptual thinking. They only exist as thoughts when they appear in our awareness; we call these appearances of thoughts our mind.

The nature of the natural mind and what we call awareness are the same thing. Awareness becomes the mind when conceptual thinking is processing information abstractly. The mind also processes information intuitively without language, especially when appearances of reality are the unmeasured perceptions of space and time; this is experienced when there are no fabrications of conceptualized ideas or measurements of either space and time, and this is experienced "as it is" when the mind is in a silent state. Space or time are conceptual experiences with no substantial existence other than what is fabricated or believed to be true conceptually.

The conceptual mind is conditioned by a reality fabricated to represent what appears and disappears in the present moment as abstract ideas. This has created a mental environment that filters and rationalizes what is experienced. We live in this mental environment conceptually, and it impacts our behavior positively and negatively.

Another aspect of the mind is separated into two entities: the conscious mind and the subconscious mind. These are:

- The conscious mind is what we experience when we are awake in the present moment. It's the state of mind experienced when we're not sleeping. It is a conscious state that is awake and self-aware. It experiences the present moment creatively, analytically, and spontaneously, with or without conceptualization.

- The subconscious mind, on the other hand, is sometimes called the "habit mind." It is hidden from the conscious mind yet always present and active. The subconscious mind doesn't sleep. It contains memories of past experiences and holds our beliefs, desires, identities, and preferences. It enables unconscious and habitual behavior, both physically and mentally, to act and react automatically.

Regarding verbal language, the mind, as we most commonly know it, exists only as thoughts. The mind doesn't exist conceptually when no thoughts or mental images appear in our awareness. Its composition is mostly a construct of language-based information, expressed as the cognitive activity of conceptual thinking. The mind we usually perceive is the appearance of concrete, and abstract thought forms in one's awareness. When awareness takes the form of conceptual thought, it becomes the mind as we typically know it. In essence, there is no conceptual mind; empty awareness prevails when thought and the conceptualization of the present moment are absent.

The Conscious Mind

The conscious mind is the part of the mind that functions and processes what I'm aware of when I'm not sleeping and am in the waking state of consciousness. It involves my immediate thoughts, perceptions, and feelings that I actively experience and can articulate when awake. The conscious mind involves my awareness of thoughts and experiences in the present moment. My utilization of language serves as a medium for expressing, sharing, and shaping those conscious experiences. I use language to convey ideas, emotions, and perceptions when I think or communicate consciously. Language provides a structure for organizing and expressing complex ideas, making it a fundamental tool for conscious thought. Language and consciousness are deeply connected.

The Verbal Environment of Language

Verbal language provides an intellectual environment that uses conceptual thought patterns and configurations that create our mental environment. Through conceptualizing thoughts, ideas, identities, beliefs, preferences, judgments, etc., this process is interfaced with the brain to develop the mind. As mentioned, its continuous thought activity occupies a mental environment in a cognitive mind space where thoughts come and go. Consciousness takes the form of verbal thoughts, creating the conceptual mind. This mind is a form of consciousness that has been concentrated dynamically to construct and express a conceptualized reality that enables human engagement and participation in a shared mental environment.

Consider that the collective mind exists within consciousness and is not confined to the body. With its thought activities, the collective mind is conceptual and not local to the body. There is a conceptual entity that I call the "mind field" that exists within consciousness and exists outside the body. The individual and collective mind are mental constructs of consciousness that conceptualize, sustain, and provide information that emerges as our thoughts through interconnectedness with the brain and the five senses. This is the dynamic aspect of consciousness taking form as thought.

When thoughts become a belief or a truth, they create a conditioned aspect unique to each person based on their experience. This conditioning abides inside consciousness, which we call the subconscious mind. Language is the instrument and interface that creates a mind that understands and communicates what it is thinking. The conceptual mind is the totality of thoughts, concepts, ideas, and abstract thinking.

How Does the Mind Know What is Real?

Your mind's experience of the present moment is limited when it succumbs to conceptualizing the experience of the present. If this is the case, you won't see the present as it is. Instead, you'll see a virtual representation of what you "think" you are experiencing, mainly related to previous conceptual knowledge and experiences. The present moment may be perceived by how your language uses thoughts to define, analyze, and describe the experience. Also, most people's present-moment experiences are biased by the conditioning of what their belief system says it is.

How we see or conceive the present moment may be overshadowed by how we want to see it. Assumptions of preconceived ideas or memories of the past may color our understanding or comprehension of present-moment experiences. These rationalizations are primarily abstract and have unsubstantiated existence in the present moment. They merely recall experiences drawn conclusively from past experiences within a mental or intellectual context.

Our memory is a mental recollection of the past - it's history! Over time, the content usually changes to become altered or a complete fabrication of what was experienced. Recent research shows that 50% of our memories have been altered or modified to suit a person's preference for what they would like them to be. Humans can rationalize what has happened or is happening to themselves. It is essential to know what the mind is and how it processes our perceptions and information.

The world as it appears and disappears in the present may be misrepresented. Thought-based phenomena have conditioned the mind to think in a specific way. However, in themselves, these thoughts have no substantial existence when related to the actual experience of the present moment.

The Thinking Mind

Some people have described the thinking mind as a "monkey mind" that persistently jumps from one thought to another. This is characterized by how one thought leads to another and exponentially creates a mental entanglement of thought activity that dominates our awareness. It's somewhat hypnotic or dream-like.

The thinking mind is similar to a map that can provide directions to locations in space and time. The map itself does not have an actual location or a timeframe. The map is symbolic and merely points one to a destination, a time, or a location in a conceptual context. It is the same with conceptual thought expressing a narrative of reality as a mental representation of "what is" or what we "think it is." The location indicated by the map cannot be experienced just by looking at the map. The map's location on paper is not the actual physical location; it only represents the location abstractly that guides us to the location in our physical environment. This is how language abstractly leads us to experience a verbal reality within this conceptual experience. It is a virtual experience or representation of what is occurring in the present moments of our lives.

Have you noticed that the thinking mind keeps us attached to our life as we "think" it to be? In this condition, we identify with pleasurable or painful experiences that have created attachments to preferences for enjoyable experiences, avoiding unpleasant ones. We are so embedded in the thinking mind that we abide by it as if it were our reality. We let it dictate our reactions, responses, and interactions within a conceptual context, mostly unconsciously. It conceals itself as an identity as if it is a thinking person. We mostly live in our minds as thoughts and beliefs.

A thinking person is the mind, using language as its source of reality. A thinking person is just that - a conceptualization of personal identities and fabricated realities that are not authentic and present an experience of the present moment that is not seen precisely as it appears. These experiences are purely symbolic images created by language that envision and project a virtual representation of a person living in a physical and mental universe. For most of us, this monkey mind never stops to rest except when we are in deep sleep.

The Mind Imagines the Past

Memories are thoughts and conceptual information stored in the brain's mental field of the subconscious mind that we can recall or remember. These stored memories are virtual impressions of what we have experienced. Memories are used to define and identify who and what we "think" we are; they are stored as imprints of conditioned thinking. This is where attachments and beliefs become actualized in our mind's conceptual imagination, creating what we call the past.

The Mind Imagines the Future

Conceptual thoughts of expectations and desires for physical and mental subjects and objects are constructs of the thought process we call our future. We can imagine what it would be like to experience or possess a subjective or objective experience in the future. Thoughts of the future have no intrinsic substance of their own. In other words, in the present moment, they are the conceptualized imaginations of the thinking mind based on our attachment to desires and expectations of what we want to happen. The future is always speculative and can be characterized by prediction, probability, and assumption.

Our desires have a futuristic aspect where the expectation of fulfilling them either brings them to fruition or causes unreal experiences and even anxiety. However, it can be helpful to envision the manifestation of one's desires by repetitively applying persistent thoughts of fulfillment to create a desired outcome.

The Subconscious Mind

The Subconscious Mind

The subconscious mind is a hidden area of consciousness below the surface of the conscious mind. It contains stored information about everything we have ever experienced, including memories, beliefs, emotions, attachments, preferences, and habitual behavior. The subconscious mind is a construct of conditioned imprinting that has been neurologically wired into the brain through habitual repetition or by conditioned attachments and beliefs. It is conditioned based on the memories of past experiences and conceptual programming. These imprints have conditioned the mind and become hidden operations below conscious awareness.

While the conscious mind is what we are currently aware of in our wakeful state, the subconscious mind is hidden from it and always works in the background, influencing how we react to things and shaping our behavior. It's like an iceberg: The subconscious is below the surface of the water, and the conscious mind is the tip of the iceberg visible above the water.

The subconscious mind is a processing and storage system:

- It holds all data related to one's past experiences. It contains what is presumed or assumed as the conscious mind's conclusions regarding what it experienced or imagined to have experienced. It is an imprint of past and repetitive experiences that are stored below the surface of the conscious mind.

- It is always listening and being aware of the conscious mind's experiences. In itself, the subconscious mind doesn't discriminate between what is real and what is unreal. It takes the truth of reality from the conscious mind's interpretations and judgments to determine its validity and then stores the conclusions as truth.

- The conscious and subconscious minds perceive whatever appears physically or mentally in the present moment. The conscious mind programs the subconscious based on what is relevant or what it thinks is real.

- The evolutionary design of the subconscious mind has a functional aspect. The subconscious mind functions to sustain our existence and navigate the complexities of life through automatic and conditioned programming. When this conditioning of the mind is implemented into the subconscious, it assumes an authoritative position for habitual and autonomous behavior.

- Physical patterns of behavior acquired through repetition can be helpful and functional. By design, they become automatic, habitual behavioral patterns. This conceptual or behavioral conditioning triggers preconditioned reactions that result in autonomic behavior that does not require conscious decision-making.

The information stored in the subconscious mind is conditioned or programmed, and some of its programming can be analogous to the instructions or algorithms stored in the hard drive of a computer's operating system. This stored information in a computer is called the computer's registry. It is also hidden from the user so it cannot be manipulated, which may cause the computer to become unusable or damaged.

Some memories are organized and behave like algorithms or mental instructions. An algorithm is a step-by-step procedure or instructions for solving a problem or accomplishing a specific task. It is a sequence of well-defined instructions that a computer or, similarly, a human can execute. They instruct us on how to interact with people and the environments we encounter. It is a predictive interactive process conditioned by how we view the world, ourselves, and others.

Our stored memories are purely subjective and create a conceptually imagined reality in our subconscious. They are fabrications conditioned to affect our behavioral responses in a more habitual and reactive mode. They may also include erroneous information that was mistaken as accurate and manifests as illusive or delusive behavior. Some of our memories could be more accurate, and some may cause miscalculations or misinformation that could negatively affect our responses to the present moment.

Science has proven that there is little or no substance in the memories themselves. They are purely conceptual. What appears in the mind as a memory is a phenomenal or virtual experience; it creates a conceptual experience that fabricates a contrived view of the present moment, resulting in a conceptual reality within the mind. Memories are conceptual ideas of what we "think" happened in our past or what we imagined happened. They don't exist in the present moment! They're conceptual and abstract thoughts that either expand awareness or contract it.

If I think of the time I was on the beach at Olon in Ecuador, I could mentally picture the vast sandy beach. I could mentally see the palm trees, the people, and the umbrella tents in my recollection. Could this be a mental experience envisioned by the mind's ability to bring images and past thoughts into the present moment in the mind to experience them virtually? Or is it an altered state of consciousness? Or both? What is actually being remembered, and can it be experienced in the present moment?

Memories don't exist because they are only virtual experiences of what we "think" we experienced. They are complete fabrications of mental processing with a recall function programmed to believe they're real. The ego and personality depend on past experiences for their existence. The ego has to have a story or a history for it to exist.

The Subconscious Mind Always Says Yes

A fascinating aspect of the subconscious mind is that it always responds to the conscious mind's condition or what information it is provided with. It always listens and takes information from the conscious mind's experiences. Whatever conclusions or judgments the conscious mind makes are automatically affirmed by the subconscious mind without discrimination. It experiences the present moment but doesn't analyze or discern what is experienced. It accepts whatever conclusions the conscious mind has made and always agrees. It has no inherent discriminating or reality processing itself. For instance, when you say, "I'm tired " or "I feel sick," it believes what you say to be true, and it always says, "Yes," you are. And, you will most likely experience what information you've provided to it at the time. It also works both ways: the subconscious mind reacts to its programs through habitual reactions and behaviors. However, it also responds to the conscious mind by believing what information comes from present-moment experiences. It doesn't know the difference between what is real or unreal.

The Programming of the Subconscious Mind

In the early years of development, i.e., approximate ages 1 through 7, the mind develops by recording everything we perceive without discretion or critical thinking. Like a perpetual recording device, it records every appearance and disappearance within one's awareness, like a mental sponge that excludes nothing. Some scientific studies propose the idea that the mind continues to develop up to the age of 35. Due to neuroplasticity, it can continue to develop into old age.

Psychology and neuroscience have revealed that up to 95% of our thinking and behavior are conceived and initiated by the subconscious mind without conscious awareness or consent. The conscious mind is approximately 5%, or a small fraction, of our understanding and mindful experience.

We think and interact throughout the day with the conscious mind's awareness and analysis of what comes and goes. But, what lies beneath the surface of our conscious mind is the controlling mechanism or the programming of information and algorithmic systems that produce most of our behavior. These controlling mechanisms and algorithms create reactionary behavior when corresponding stimuli come from our experiences of subjective or objective reality.

Conditioning or programming the subconscious mind is done in several ways. For instance, if you had an impactful experience that was extremely painful, you may have stored that experience as a negative experience. Then, through rationalization, the mind determines a conclusive decision regarding its impact. The mind subconsciously programs this information, creating an avoidance or acceptance pattern through conditioned decision-making. When triggered by similar present-moment experiences, it has a pre-recorded response, programmed to respond as a reaction.

Another way the subconscious mind can be programmed or conditioned is through repetition and memorizing specific physical or mental actions until they become automatic. These are designed habit patterns that provide automatic behavior or outcomes, both physically and mentally.

These types of conditioning, whether pleasurable or painful, are transformed into what we call the past. They are conceptualized experiences of mental and physical conditioning that become habitual and automatic. Also, conscious repetitive conditioning can form habitualized patterns of thought, identity, or actions.

For example:

- Pleasurable experiences that occur repetitively and have a high value of fulfillment can condition the subconscious to create desires to attract those experiences repeatedly.

- Repetitive information or misinformation programs the subconscious to create beliefs or attachments. This could also happen by a manipulative source.

- Repetitive visualization of seeing an outcome as fulfilled can manifest the desired result.

- Repetitive verbal affirmations can create programmed emotions and feelings in the subconscious mind in a positive way.

Physical Conditioning of the Habit Mind

Physically, conditioning the subconscious mind to acquire and sustain motor skills is achieved using repetitive muscle motor-memory practices or techniques. These create conditioned actions that manifest automatic behavior without conscious attention. An example of this is the skill of a basketball player to make consistent, successful shots through the basketball hoop.

As a trained musician, I developed technical skills to attain and acquire muscle motor-memory proficiency in developing fingering patterns, articulation, and interpretive expression. These skills were programmed physically and mentally through intense, repetitive practice and "unconscious memorization." This process accomplishes most skills requiring motor memory.

An exciting aspect of conditioning or re-conditioning mental or physical proficiencies is the methods and processes utilized in the programming. As a musician, what I found that obstructs or delays development in mental and physical programming is that the amount of information is too overwhelming and, therefore, cannot be processed by the mind efficiently or accurately. For instance, unsuccessful attempts to execute a difficult technical passage only result in programming the unsuccessful attempts into the subconscious mind. This results in continued failures and frustration. These erroneous experiences must be deprogrammed to attain the correct and accurate information, physically and mentally. A waste of time!

Physical programming can be effortless if organized into smaller, isolated segments. These can be cognized and physiologically programmed with little effort because mental and physical computation is attainable.

Accurate mental comprehension of the proposed task should precede any attempt to execute it physically. Conditioning of the mental programming should precede any physical action or communication of the physical requirements.

For example, when you integrate the body and mind to coordinate the physical and mental components required to perform a complex piece of music or a dancer to execute a complicated choreography, there has to be a systematic way of attaining this coordination. Attempted execution of the task must be experienced correctly every time to program the required coordination into the psycho-physical experience. If an overwhelming amount of information is attempted and every attempt to accomplish the task fails, mental and physical efforts must be scaled down into smaller components for accurate implementation. Physical or psychological information must be communicated from the brain to the body to connect the neurological wiring that coordinates the motor functions.

For example, when you were taught how to put your clothes on every day, you practiced this to complete the various tasks until you were successful. You may not remember learning this task because it became automatic, and you didn't have to think or learn how to do it every time you put your clothes on.

It may be required to slow the process down so that a successful learning practice ensues. This is done by communicating to the body and mind with perfect mental or physical information. I use a metronome to incrementally accomplish the desired result when practicing music to acquire physical technique. In other words, I can slow the tempo of the exercise to a speed at which my mind can comprehend and execute the exercise with precision and accuracy. Therefore, I can program the exercise by incrementally speeding up the tempo so that it never becomes impossible and is never perceived as difficult. By using this method, the desired speed is accomplished.

Working as an Occupational Therapist taught me to break down "activities of daily living" into small tasks or actions so the mind can focus on less information and communication. This entailed a series of sequential learning tasks that were initiated step-by-step to install the correct information into the brain to accomplish each task. This process also enables the assimilation of information into successful sequences that eventually achieve the entire task. This was most helpful in treating stroke or neurologically impaired patients.

Occupational therapeutic techniques came naturally to me because of my intense study of music. The same principles of learning and programming apply in life. Slowing things down and being conscious of the present moment are essential to living effortlessly in the flow of life.

Behavioral Consequences of Subconscious Conditioning

Because of subconscious conditioning, the attempt to create positive change in behaviors or fulfill many desires may not be possible due to previous conditioning that stands firm in maintaining a status quo even though the change may benefit one's well-being. An example of this is when one is addicted to some food or dessert, which is a mental condition. One can consciously attempt to control the desire to discontinue the addiction, but it will persist due to its programming in the subconscious mind. Hacking into the subconscious and eliminating the programming will take mental work. Here again, awareness is critical. It is possible to change or modify the subconscious programs of the mind. Still, it takes commitment, intention, and understanding to persist in correcting the information and the conditioned attachments. The inability to alter or change the subconscious mind is all due to the already programmed conditioning of stored behavior inaccessible to the conscious mind. Successful programming cannot be done if the preconditioned mental and physical information is inaccessible. Because the subconscious is hidden, these algorithms can't be modified or changed easily. It is possible to deprogram the subconscious mind, which will become apparent as we proceed.

Another example of subconscious conditioning is when one drives and gets lost in thought, not paying attention to the task. Several miles down the road, one becomes aware and attentive to the task and can't even remember who or what was driving the vehicle. Fortunately, the subconscious mind was driving on autopilot while this was happening.

The subconscious mind can affect behavior in many ways, for example:

- Habits and Patterns: The subconscious mind is responsible for the formation and execution of habits and patterns. It stores information about our daily routines and automates repetitive actions, allowing us to perform tasks without conscious effort. Riding a bicycle is an example.

- Beliefs and Values: Our subconscious mind holds our beliefs and values, which can significantly influence our behavior. These beliefs and values are often formed through past experiences and conditioning, shaping our perception of the world and guiding our actions.

- Emotional Responses: The subconscious mind also plays a significant role in our emotional responses. It stores emotional memories and associations, triggering emotional reactions to certain situations or stimuli.

- Decision-Making: The subconscious mind also influences our decision-making and creative processes. It can provide intuitive insights and guide us toward choices based on past experiences and stored information.

- Problem-Solving: When exploring ideas and trying to find a solution to a problem, the subconscious mind works in the background to find an answer or to discover a solution as long as the mind persists in the inquiry. A solution may take several days or years to come to fruition. Scientists experience this with their many experiments.

Our subconscious mind holds our self-image and self-perception, which can impact our behavior and interactions with others. A negative self-image can lead to self-sabotaging behaviors, while a positive self-image can boost confidence and motivation. These thoughts and images create the ego, fabricated through the conceptual realities we have conditioned.

It's important to note that while the subconscious mind significantly impacts behavior, this doesn't mean we have no control over our actions. The subconscious mind's language is empirically constructed based on our traumas and repetitive experiences. Conditioned behaviors can be changed or modified by becoming aware of them.

The Subconscious Mind is Where Identities and Feelings Are Stored

The subconscious mind holds a conceptual knowledge of who you believe yourself to be. Based on these beliefs, a personality is developed. Your self-agent and self-image interact with the world and all the personal experiences you have or have ever had. This identity is stored in the subconscious mind and is mainly hidden from conscious awareness. However, it projects its conditioned persona to react to the present moment in a prefabricated manner, which can be observed.

Emotions and feelings that have been repetitively experienced and have gained some value, either positively or negatively, are also programmed into the subconscious mind.

Some examples are:

- How one feels about one's health and what is essential to maintain it is stored in the subconscious as patterns of opinions that influence behavior.

- Painful and pleasurable experiences are conditioned feelings programmed into the subconscious. When triggered by present-moment experiences, they display their impact by expressing behavior in specific ways of attraction or repulsion.

- Psychological states such as depression or bipolar disorder are conditions of either chemical dysfunctions or subconscious programming. These states are stored in the subconscious.

- Personality traits such as pride, jealousy, hate, racism, etc., may be imprinted into the subconscious mind, as well.

- Moral and ethical experiences create emotions that are also contained in the subconscious due to the programming of conceptualized ideologies and beliefs.

In summary, if you are awake, alert, and conscious of this internal interaction between the conscious and subconscious minds, you can choose what to think and believe is happening in the present moment. You can be freed of the conditioned content of the subconscious mind if you become aware of them and exercise a detachment or dispassionate association with your thoughts. You won't be manipulated by unconscious actions that are not in your best interest. Also, this freedom enables you to see what is real and what is not. You can also change any situation immediately for your well-being. This is important and the key to always being happy, loving, and kind.

You Can Hack Into the Subconscious Mind and Change Its Contents

Habitual thinking and behavior create experiences that wire our brains to think in a specific way. Most people are unaware of this and take this process for granted. This leads one to believe this is "the way things are" or "this is who I am." We can rewire our thoughts and weed out memories that no longer serve us.

The subconscious can be reprogrammed through self-awareness, attentive intention, and conscious effort. Through these, the subconscious can be modified or rewired. When the mind is silenced, thoughts and behavioral conditioning appear and are seen in the empty awareness as they arise. You can make changes once you know what is hidden in the subconscious. As I said, awareness is the key. By understanding and harnessing the power of your subconscious mind, you can make the necessary changes to alter your behavior and improve your well-being.

Discovering what is dictating your behavior from what has been conditioned in the subconscious mind is easy. When you commit yourself to observing your behavior consciously and intentionally, you become aware of the conditioned programming of the subconscious mind. Observing your behavior as it is experienced in the activities of daily living, you become aware of your reactions and responses. Intentional observation and becoming aware of your thoughts and behavior will reveal everything you need to know about what is programmed in the subconscious mind. Your reactionary behavior, both physically and mentally, will reveal your subconscious programming. Through awareness and observation, these conditions are exposed. Once seen for what they are, they can be eliminated or defused. They will no longer keep you trapped in habitual thoughts or actions.

Releasing subconscious conditioning can be a monumental task for which most of us are unwilling to do or have the psychological stamina. Delving deep into the dark recesses of your mind may reveal many negative imprints that you may not wish to experience again. It all comes down to letting go of all and any attachments to memories or concepts of the past. By doing so, you diffuse its energy. It is essential to let go of the past. You must also forgive anyone or anything that has caused a negative experience in your mind. You can also thank anyone or any situation for allowing you to experience something painful, hurtful, embarrassing, abusive, deceitful, or harmful. These experiences have molded you to become who you are today. Being grateful for having these experiences also diffuses the energy in your mind as you become aware of them and see them for what they are with an empty mind.

Conclusively, the conscious and subconscious mind is a phenomenal experience that doesn't have an existential reality outside of conceptualization and imagination. The totality of the mind is fictitious by its very nature and should be exposed as a simulation of one's life, as in a game or a sport. Without conceptual thought created by language and the mental activity of thinking, the conceptualized aspect of the mind subsides naturally.

The mind is like a field of awareness full of conceptual thought that has fabricated a conceptual reality that doesn't have any substantial authenticity in the present moment. In its natural state, the mind is like a blank movie screen with nothing projected onto it until an image appears—it's just a blank, empty screen! Once an image or story is projected onto the screen, it seems as if it is real, or we have an imaginative experience of an objective reality that can be experienced there.

If an image of an ocean is projected onto the screen, the screen doesn't get wet. If the movie's narrative has emotional content that affects us emotionally, its projection onto the screen doesn't make it real even though we experience it as if it is.

The Subconscious Mind is a Fabrication of the Past

If you become aware of an impression of a memory abiding in your consciousness, it becomes apparent that it doesn't exist in the present moment. It is a past imprint that has no substance at all in the present moment. It's history! But, it can continue to appear and control your behavior as if it is happening in the present experience. Once aware, it ceases to operate as a reactionary impulse if it is diffused whenever it appears.

"Abiding in the Present Moment" is essential to reprogramming the subconscious. If awareness is empty of conceptual thought, the present-moment experience transcends any subconscious programming.

The present moment is where everything happens! Nothing can happen in the past (it's gone) or the future (it's not here), as neither can manifest in the present moment. All that exists is the present moment. The future is only a possibility that is not guaranteed to provide a desired outcome. If you want to change or create anything in your life, your attention or intention should abide in the present moment, where everything is happening and is possible.

VERBAL & NON-VERBAL REALITY

Conceptually, you can experience the past through your thoughts and imagination. Still, no reality emerges from it in the present moment other than a conceptual one which can never be experienced as it was initially. You can plan future events or experiences which may or may not come to fruition. Nothing is guaranteed.

The language and thought content we are using in the present moment allows all potentials of these thoughts to be actualized. You may be misguided or misrepresented by your conceptual thinking, and the consequences may be harmful. The mind is a tool created primarily by verbal language; without this, it doesn't exist conceptually. You must use it properly to see clearly and know what is real and what is not as you experience the present.

"An empty mind" is synonymous with empty awareness, meaning that no phenomenal appearances exist conceptually in the mind or awareness. Empty awareness prevails as the ground of our existence without conceptual thinking. Self-awareness is sustained by the field of consciousness, which is the same as the field of awareness. Awareness becomes the mind when the conceptualization of reality appears and is experienced as if it is real.

Awareness is likened to an unconditioned space where all experiences and possibilities can form, like the quantum field. It is experienced as the presence of existence itself or a quantum field of possibilities and probabilities that differentiate a conceptual mind from an empty mind. Like energy, consciousness transforms into multitudes of forms. All creation exists as consciousness with or without form. It became apparent that consciousness is the only thing that exists; all creation appears when consciousness takes form.

This is the most critical aspect of self-discovery, and it is fundamental! If you don't know what the mind is, you will live a life of ignorance, illusions, or delusions as to what is real or not real.

Chapter 4

Emotions and Feelings

Emotions are complex psychological and physiological states that arise in response to stimuli or situations. They involve subjective feelings, thoughts, and physiological changes like heart rate, facial expressions, and hormonal levels. Emotions can be categorized into various basic types: joy, anger, fear, sadness, disgust, etc.. They play a crucial role in the human experience, influencing behavior, decision-making, and social interactions.

Emotions can also be challenging at times. For example, thinking clearly or making good decisions can be difficult if you experience strong negative emotions like anger or sadness. Language and emotion are closely intertwined aspects of the human experience that affect our behavior. They can influence each other in many ways, both directly and indirectly.

Language Can Affect Our Emotions.

Language influences how we perceive and interpret situations. Language describes situations that can shape our emotional response to them. For example, describing a situation as "threatening" or "dangerous" makes us more likely to feel fearful. On the other hand, describing a problem as "challenging" or "exciting" makes us more likely to feel motivated.

Language can influence how we express and understand our emotions. It allows us to label and communicate our feelings to others. It also helps us make sense of our emotions and develop coping mechanisms.

In other words, language influences how we regulate our emotions. We can use language to create thoughts to calm ourselves down when we are feeling anxious or angry or to boost our mood when we are feeling down. We can also use language to regulate the emotions of others.

Emotion Can Affect Our Language

Emotions can influence our choice of words and grammar. When we are feeling strong emotions, we may use more intense language. For example, someone feeling angry might say, "I'm furious!" instead of "I'm angry."

Emotions can influence our ability to communicate effectively. Strong emotions can make it difficult to express our thoughts and feelings clearly and coherently. Emotions can also affect our willingness to communicate. We may be less likely to communicate with others when we feel ashamed or embarrassed.

Emotions and language are two inextricably linked aspects of the human experience. They can affect our behavior in several ways, both directly and indirectly. By understanding how emotions and language interact, we can learn to use language to support our emotional well-being.

What Are Feelings and How Does Language Affect Them?

Feelings are the conscious experience of our awareness of emotions. They are the subjective experience of the emotional response that involves cognitive interpretation and have a personal significance. Feelings are more reflective and involve a higher level of mental processing.

Emotions are automatic and physiological responses, while feelings are conscious experiences and interpretations of those responses. The correlation lies in the fact that feelings arise from our emotions, and our conscious awareness of emotions is what we commonly refer to as feelings. The relationship between them is intricate and complex.

Emotions serve as the underlying foundation for our conscious experience. They arise from our interaction with the world and ourselves, reflecting our interpretations and evaluations of situations. On the other hand, feelings are personal and unique, varying in intensity and nuance depending on individual experiences and perspectives. Physiological responses can occur as feelings often accompany bodily changes like heart rate fluctuations, muscle tension, and hormonal shifts.

Regarding motivation and action, feelings guide our thoughts, behaviors, and interactions with the world. Feelings are transient; while some might linger, they generally come and go over time.

Understanding feelings is an ongoing pursuit in psychology and neuroscience. We know they involve intricate brain networks, but pinpointing their origins and mechanisms remains challenging.

Verbal Language Dances with Feelings

Language plays a fascinating and multifaceted role in our emotional tapestry. We name and identify our feelings with words, which label feelings to help us recognize and differentiate them. This labeling process activates brain regions involved in emotion and language, suggesting a close intertwining.

Language can shape our perceptions. The words we use to describe things influence how we perceive and experience them. For instance, framing something as "challenging" rather than "threatening" can alter our emotional response.

When we share our feelings through language, it connects us to others, fostering empathy and understanding. Talking about your feelings can also help you process and regulate the experience. Languages vary in emotional vocabularies, suggesting cultural differences in how emotions are categorized and understood. Language helps construct your feelings.

Language is a powerful tool for understanding, navigating, and sharing one's emotional world. It shapes how one perceives, expresses, and experiences feelings, making it a key player in the ever-intriguing dance between mind and emotion.

Physical Sensation vs. Emotional Feelings

There's a difference between "feeling something" and "emotional feelings," which can be approached from a few angles, depending on the context. Feeling something usually refers to experiencing a physical sensation perceived through your five senses. This is physical. For example, feeling the sun's warmth on your skin, the taste of a delicious meal, or the tickle of a feather. These sensations are immediate and concrete, arising directly from sensory input. However, emotional feelings typically refer to happiness, sadness, anger, fear, etc. These are more of a mental activity or mental process that defines their expression.

Emotions are more complex and involve sensory input, thoughts, interpretations, and physiological responses. They can last longer than physical sensations and be influenced by internal and external factors.

Feeling something generally refers to a singular, specific sensation at a given moment. You might be feeling cold, tired, or excited. However, feelings can refer to a broader range of emotional states that fluctuate over time. For example, you might feel love for your family, anxiety about a presentation, or overall emotional well-being.

It's important to note that these are not strict classifications, and there can be overlap between "feeling something" and "feelings." For example, feeling a tight knot in your stomach can be both a physical sensation and an indicator of anxiety. Likewise, excitement about an upcoming trip can involve emotional anticipation and physical changes like increased heart rate.

Ultimately, the meaning depends on the context and word use. Here are several examples:

- You may use tentative and hesitant language if you feel anxious about a job interview. For example, you might think or say, "I think I might be able to do this" instead of "I know I can do this."

- You might use more aggressive and accusatory language when angry at a friend. For example, you might say, "You always do this to me!" instead of "I'm feeling hurt because of what you did."

- If you feel sad about a loss, you may use more reflective and introspective language. For example, you might say, "I'm still trying to process what happened," instead of "I can't believe this is happening to me."

By being mindful of your language and how it affects your emotions and feelings, you can learn to communicate more effectively and appropriately manage them.

Language's emotional conditioning is conditioned as a subordinate reality matrix superimposed on our experiences through habitual use. We communicate to ourselves and others about how we feel in the same way that our thought processes express to others what we experience in the present moments of our lives.

Chapter 5: The Ego & Personality

Chapter 5

The Ego and Personality

What is Ego?

The ego is a complex fabrication of conceptual ideas and beliefs that create a person's identity, attachments, desires, and beliefs through a verbal matrix made up in the mind. The mind imagines it as a mental field of energy occupying a mental space that functions as a personal existence separate from everything else. It behaves as an independent agent apart from any other existing thing. It is the individual identity of an imagined person, a complex mental structure of conceptual ideas that humans "think" of themselves. It is a complete and virtual representation of a fabricated avatar attached to the appearance of a body and mind in a conceptualized reality.

The ego personality is always engaged or entangled in what the senses perceive and what is cognized by the mind. Due to conditioning, the ego differentiates and discerns what the mind assimilates intellectually. Our conditioned attachments to positive or negative thinking impact our subjective and objective experiences of ourselves and the world. These patterns of thinking create specific outcomes of reality experiences. Scrutinizing the nature of language and conceptual thinking was a significant discovery, helping me to know who I am and what is not real.

The ego plays a significant role in our lives. Just as an actor plays a role in a performance, it plays a role in one's life as a personal agent, a construct of thoughts regarding identities, emotions, and feelings. It associates itself with the body and is attached to it as its residence. The idea of a person is a subjective experience that humans believe to be true about themselves. However, in absolute reality, there is no ego or person to be identified with when language and conceptual thinking are suspended.

You can feel the ego's presence as you "think" and "believe" that you exist. Your language forms the existence of much of your identity. This creates conceptual ideas and beliefs about who and what you perceive as the body and mind. This identity factor is the main limitation that affects a person's experience of what's real and what's inaccurate as they interact with physical and mental environments subjectively and objectively.

The ego only exists as an experience of your thought processing. It's formed by memories of your past experiences regarding who and what you know about your assumed self. It is a self-centered creation that is a virtual experience of your imagination. You and your acceptance of what others have told you about yourself have created it.

The ego experiences itself through the association with the body as its residence. It uses language, processed by the brain, to create it conceptually as the egoic mind of an imaginary person. The ego's mind is believed to be real. It is all made up like a character in a play. It imagines itself as the performer who then thinks, feels, and believes itself as a person. Is there a person that exists as an independent self, or is it just made-up thoughts of who you "think" you are?

The ego experiences its existence as if it is conscious of itself. It has a self-conscious aspect of knowing itself. It compels one to "think" it has an existence or an identity as a separate person.

In reality, it has no existential qualities that intrinsically provide any substantial existence that is real. It is entirely conceptual and has developed over a lifetime of experiences and behavioral conditioning experienced habitually, and most people are unaware of its illusion.

We are taught that we are this body. That thought allows the emergence of conceptual identities and beliefs to become associated with the body as its physical vehicle and the thinking mind as its mental body. Conceptual identities and beliefs are only possible through conceptual thinking and identification with the body as if the experience of the body and mind make up the person. You are much more than that! And you are not a body or a mind , you only "think" you are.

The egoic experience also associates itself with emotions and the sensation of feelings. It experiences the perceptions of life through the body, and the mind conceptually processes those sensations. This is what gives it a sense of being real. But if you look into its source, it is only sensational experiences of the body that are conceptualized by the mind. The ego continually wants to validate its existence, but all the while, it is an imaginary one. It is essential to see through these identifications and realize that the ego is not your true self and doesn't reside in your body.

The idea of a personal existence is perpetrated by societal, cultural, and personal conditioning. Individually and collectively, your personality is a matrix of thoughts of who you "think" you are and who you were told that you are. Most people abide by it as if it's real. What would exist as you if the ideas of who you are were eliminated from your mind? If all thoughts of who you are were suspended, would you disappear into nothingness? Could you abide in this silent and empty space as your fundamental Self?

It's not my intention to negate the ego or relinquish its importance. It serves its purpose if we interact with the appearances in our subjective and objective realities. Becoming free of the ego's attachments, identities, and beliefs is essential! It requires observation, detachment, and dissociation from it as far as believing it is real or providing a genuine identity. This dispassion enables us to see what is real about our existence and how we can freely choose our behavior as appearances and disappearances of reality come and go.

Archetypes

Carl Jung proposed the concept of archetypes, which are universal, inherited patterns or images that reside in the collective unconscious of all humans. These archetypes influence our thoughts, feelings, and behaviors, and they can be found in myths, stories, dreams, and art across cultures and throughout history.

Here are some examples of Jung's archetypes:

- The Persona: The persona is the mask we wear in social situations. It's the face we present to the world that conforms to social expectations and helps us fit in. It can be our professional persona, our family persona, or our friend persona.

- The Shadow: The shadow is the part of ourselves that we repress or reject. It contains our negative qualities, our dark desires, and our instincts. We often push the shadow into the unconscious because it's uncomfortable or unacceptable. But according to Jung, it's important to integrate the shadow into our personality to become whole.

- The Anima/Animus: The anima is the feminine archetype in a man's unconscious, and the animus is the masculine archetype in a woman's unconscious. These archetypes represent the opposite sex and can influence our relationships with others. For example, a man might project his anima onto a woman he finds attractive, or a woman might project her animus onto a man she admires.

- The Self: The self is the archetypal center of the personality. It represents our wholeness, our unity, and our potential for individuation. Jung believed that the goal of life is to become our authentic selves and integrate all of our archetypes into a harmonious whole.

- The Hero: The hero is a common archetype in myths and stories. The hero is typically a courageous individual who overcomes challenges and defeats evil. This archetype can inspire us to face our own challenges and live our lives to the fullest.

These are just a few examples of Carl Jung's archetypes. He identified many other archetypes, each of which can be interpreted differently. By understanding archetypes, we can better understand ourselves, our ego, and others and see the universal patterns that connect us all. Personality traits can be learned, whereas archetypes are the basic fabric of our personality.

Besides the archetypes, people can simultaneously have multiple personality traits in their psychological realm. For example, one's occupational identity can be a learned identity that emerges over time as a personality trait. One may have additional traits that are empathic or spiritual, and all of these can coexist simultaneously. The personality traits that predominate in one's ego are persistently the predominating mechanism of behavior. Many inherent traits are inherited by thousands of years of human evolution, where genetic structures, such as DNA, are passed down from generation to generation.

The ego is complex and is not necessarily a negative human characteristic. There's nothing wrong with imagining oneself as an ego or a person. It's okay to be an actor in this playground of existence. It's a primary function necessary to interact, navigate, and stay alive in this multi-dimensional reality as long as we have a body. The most problematic issue with the ego is when a person is unaware and unconscious of its existence.

However, there is a natural state of being that is not defined conceptually and is aware of itself.

This authentic self is natural and hasn't been conceptualized with a personal identity or existence. It is spontaneously empty, void of history, expectations, or assumptions.

The main problem with the ego is its attachment to an imaginary identity and belief system. Suppose you are unaware that your ego and personality are fictitious. In that case, you are not awakened to your true Self; the underlying ground of consciousness is beyond your ego. The authentic Self is the unidentified and undefined awareness you were born with.

We can play a role in this life without an attachment to being identified or defined as a person with a personal identity or a defined personality with a history. Our authentic self can effortlessly play a role in the environments we experience with our body and mind. Once we stop conceptualizing everything with words and thoughts, we seamlessly flow in the energies that emerge as our present moment. The body is connected and is part of the present-moment appearances; the body is not separate from these appearances. It belongs to this physical matrix that we experience sensationally, psychologically, and emotionally. What is essential is being aware that your ego exists and that you have developed various identities and beliefs that either serve your best interest or are possibly sabotaging you. The authentic Self is beyond the body or mind; it was never born and can never die. It is what many refer to as the Absolute!

In summary, if you are unaware, your egoic identity will control you, and your thoughts will define you. Your attachments and preferences will determine your behavior and trigger the subconscious mind to behave automatically without your awareness. If you are unaware of it, you will be unable to control it. It's not hopeless! As we continue our discourse, you will see how to stop identifying yourself as an imaginary person.

The Spiritual or Religious Ego

Most spiritual seekers acquire a spiritual or religious ego, especially during the transition phase of stepping into a spiritual path. They already have a programmed view of their past and a past image of themselves. This transition to a new spiritual identity seems to require that one transforms one's identity into a spiritual one.

If a spiritual seeker joins a path, religion, or spiritual practice, it is common for them to dress and act appropriately for the collective image of their selected group. The aspirant will copy the group's cosmetic appearance and basic lifestyle. This is common and seems to be necessary in most cases.

The spiritual ego may become an obstacle to one's spiritual growth. For instance, if there is a multi-level hierarchical structure for group members to advance their status of spiritual attainment, the aspirant may fall prey to false imaginations of their spiritual identity. In Zen Buddhism, one can advance one's status and title by doing a specific number of intense meditative practices or solving a hundred or so Koans (incomprehensible riddles that stop conceptual thinking). These practices may be valid, but in some cases, they may be just another ego identification of one attaining a status above others. It should be the reverse of this.

Another example is when the ego acquires a status that provides a belief that they have attained the highest spiritual level and then acclaims themselves to be awakened or enlightened. This is a massive illusion on the spiritual path that doesn't end well. This is the ego taking on a false spiritual identity misguided by thinking and believing that they have become awakened or enlightened. This is also a conceptual experience that cannot be substantiated. So, when the aspirant misconstrues this, an ego attachment emerges and becomes a sustained idea or belief in their mind. This ego attachment can be an obstacle and prolong realization, especially when one claims they are now a Guru or a teacher.

Also, some desire to become gurus or teachers, and their goal is to have many followers. They hold classes, lectures, and write books. By their intellectual understanding of scriptures and spiritual practices, they develop a persona that may give the impression that they have become realized or awakened. This is the false Guru or teacher. If someone says they are awakened, enlightened, or self-realized, take it with a grain of salt. Most likely, they have a well-refined, believable ego.

As the aspirant progresses and has had some spiritual insights, the mind can get entangled in attempting to re-experience a past spiritual experience. Unfortunately, the seeker never finds what they seek because the seeker and what is being sought is the same thing, and nothing can be seen or attained by the mind. One should always be aware that the ego is trying to become enlightened. This is the most fundamental realization in the practice of self-awakening and probably the most difficult to overcome. The ego does not want to relinquish its autonomy or control and persistently hides its presence as it assumes a role and identity as being you, the person who is trying to attain spiritual enlightenment.

After years of spiritual practice and seeking, the aspirant matures in his spiritual endeavors and begins to understand that this practice of seeking is futile. In searching for enlightenment, they have gone down one rabbit hole after another, resulting in a dead end every time. These experiences exhaust the mind intellectually, as all attempts are unsuccessful. Eventually, one simply gives up and begins to let go of the conceptualized self and settles into an empty state of mind and awareness where there are no beliefs or identities. This is the initial and authentic awakening or enlightened state. It is the opposite of a conditioned self that was fabricated by conceptualization. This is the authentic Self that is always present, all the time.

Surrendering the Ego - Letting Go

The ego is a remarkably elusive aspect of the mind that seems determined not to be discovered. It has a personality of its own (Ha!). If you try to see or find your ego, your ego says, "Let me help you." So, it begins by looking at who, what, where, and when you are experiencing yourself as a person with identities, attachments, and beliefs. Can the ego monitor itself to confirm that it exists or doesn't? Who or what is trying to see or surrender the ego? Who is trying to let go of the ego? Is it possible that the ego is trying to surrender itself to become an enlightened being? Can you find the ego? And who is trying to find the ego? Is the ego trying to find itself? There are no correct conceptual answers to these questions, as they are purely conceptual.

There's nothing to let go of. Looking deeply inside your mind, you won't find a real ego. It's all made up in your mind, a mental environment of conceptualized experiences and thoughts that create and sustain a language-based fabrication of yourself, your life, and your reality. When you realize this, your life is transformed into a pure state of "being" known as the Absolute reality beyond the dualities of language and what the mind thinks.

How Do You Experience the Present Moment as an Egoless Person?

Many people have had experiences where they are aware of the self as not being an imagined person, or they have experienced an understanding of an egoless self. Some have even gone beyond that and have experienced a fully awakened state. Many people have these experiences when they are on psychedelic drugs, but they cannot sustain these states, and they subside when the drug subsides. One can abide in a silent "presence of being" as one's primary identity without the assistance of drug-induced substances or spiritual practices. This is a natural state of being that is not conceptual or intellectual. It is not codependent upon anything other than its pure "being."

Humans have been conditioned for thousands of years to exist in this phenomenon in a most complex and unnatural way. The attachment to the identity of being a person with a body is the ego problem. When this attachment is relinquished, there's a silent knowing of who you are that is not defined or characterized by any conceptual idea of the thinking mind. This is a state of unknowing or not knowing who you are. It is paradoxical in the sense that I know who I am, and I don't know who I am simultaneously. You don't know who you are when the mind has been silenced. When the mind knows who you are, it is "thinking" that it knows who you are and is in a fabricated conceptual state of intellectual constructs. Without thoughts, the mind doesn't exist, conceptually. If you can be comfortable not knowing who you are and see any idea of who you are as false or irrelevant, you will see clearly and have a silent understanding of what is and what is not or who you are and who you are not.

Experience and acceptance of the present moment exactly as it appears can only be achieved if conceptual thinking has been suspended. This is a pure state of awareness that is empty of conceptual thought. The present moment doesn't exist as a thought or a concept. Thoughts are fabricated ideas regarding all appearances and disappearances that come and go.

The idea "I am" is a concept that comes closest to describing who and what one is in Absolute reality. The words "I am" are the self-evident knowledge that you exist. All people know they exist - it's a default state of intuitive knowing. The ego and the world come into existence when the "I am" is assigned a predicate. Example: "I am a nice person. I am a bad person." When you are only "I am," you are none of these. Stay as "I am" and let go of all fabrications that define or describe "I am."

Chapter 6: Dualistic Thinking

Chapter 6

Verbal Language Creates Dualistic Thinking

Yin Yang

"Yin Yang" is the Taoist concept of dualistically viewing appearances and experiences as subjects having their opposites, such as light and dark, hot and cold, and each has a polarized attraction/repulsion aspect. This view is conditioned by a language matrix, as well. It is polaristic by attraction and repulsion characteristics, similar to the electromagnetic forces of the universe, which have positive and negative polarity. The thinking mind abides in this polarity of attraction and repulsion, and it has a paradoxical nature that will become evident as we look deeper.

The Chinese Taoist religion categorizes the feminine aspect of the universe with the word "Yin" and the masculine element with the word

"Yang." The Yin and Yang polarity are present in all of creation. It is said that the entire creation of existence emerges from these two aspects, and nothing would come into existence if they were not present. An infinite spectrum of subjects and objects exists in this polarization of existence from the negative (Yin) to the positive (Yang). Nothing is totally Yin or Yang. A spectrum of factors determines which will predominate and function polaristically.

The Polarity of Dualistic Thinking

Our language is dualistic, inherently. Almost every concept has a positive and negative aspect that imposes dualistic concepts such as black and white, good and bad, hot and cold, pleasure or pain, etc.

This limited thinking process constricts or contracts consciousness to adhere to these conditions. Thinking this way can be problematic when you exclusively take one side of the polarity. It limits your experience and blinds you from the opposite side of experience. It confines one to a specific form of limited consciousness that may not be true or may not be in your best interest. If you are positive, your negative side is automatically confirmed and present, or vice versa. Yin confirms the existence of Yang, and

Yang confirms the existence of Yin. When you take one side of the equation, it also validates the other side.

Thus, what we create in our dualistic thinking simultaneously takes on positive and negative qualities and consequences. When one is emotionally focused on one side, the attraction to the other is imminent. For instance, if someone is fixated on themselves contracting a horrible disease, the action of being afraid of it and the emotional experience caused by this fear attracts the very thing that one is afraid of. Vicious cycles are created that are entrapments that keep one from being balanced and in a state of well-being. The only way to free yourself from this dilemma is to be conscious of not getting attached to either side as being absolute. This affords one to see clearly as to what choices one should make. When one sees everything as it is, more clarity and understanding follow. It is essential to allow the negative aspects of reality to be part of your conscious experience. You don't have to get attached to them.

To go beyond the dualities and see everything "as it is" is not our natural way of seeing things due to our conditioning. Therefore, it is unlikely that this will occur naturally. It will take effort with much intention, awareness, and contemplation to overcome this duality-based experience. Once again, awareness is the key to liberating one from this dualism.

However, it is crucial to see the whole picture. Although, it may be logical and appropriate to take one side over the other. By consciously choosing and being aware of its consequences, we can align ourselves with its dualistic conditions. It's all about being conscious and awakened to an unattached mind that is not defining or identifying anything as being this or that. You can live within the dualities and not be attached to them one way or the other.

The Law of Attraction

The "Law of Attraction" is also based on these dynamics of Yin attracting Yang and vice versa. In the early '60s, I followed a traditional Japanese diet called "Macrobiotics." Every food item was characterized as either a Yin or Yang food. It even went further than that, including the climate, temperature, activities, and personality traits. It was a well-defined regimen of categorization that made a lot of sense and still does in modern times.

For example, if you lived in a tropical or hot climate (Yang), you would automatically be drawn to eat tropical fruits (Yin) in your diet as a natural consequence of balance. This would balance the Yin/Yang polarity and provide a complimentary diet for that environment. However, if you ate a very Yang diet in a Yang climate, you might experience illness or disease if you ate this way for a long time.

Another example is that if you lived in the Arctic like the Eskimos, you would be in a very Yin climate with no vegetation available. Therefore, animal flesh, like seafood, would be a natural food source for that climate. You wouldn't be attracted to fruits in this climate, either. Thus, balancing the Yin/Yang polarity according to the climate and environment occurs naturally if you eat what is grown in your environment.

If your constitution were extreme at any time, either a Yin or a Yang constitution, you would attract the opposite conditions at the same level of intensity, which could also be extreme. The idea is to balance Yin and Yang, avoiding any extremes, so you stay in the middle of both to narrow its energetic consequences for good health and mental clarity.

Chapter 7

The Language of Mathematics

What is Mathematics?

Mathematics is used to model, quantify, and analyze the world. It provides a framework for understanding and solving problems in various fields, from physics and engineering to finance and social sciences. It's the area of knowledge concerned with the logic of shape, quantity, and arrangement. It explores structures and abstractions, focusing on their properties and relationships. It also studies patterns and relationships independent of their physical manifestation, and it can be used to represent theories about empirical reality. Imagine the world like a giant puzzle, full of clues and patterns hidden in plain sight. Math is the magical key that unlocks those secrets! Here are some examples:

- Mathematics Speaks a Universal Language: Unlike other languages, math uses numbers and symbols that everyone understands, no matter where they come from. It's like having a secret code that works everywhere!

- Mathematics makes sense of things. Have you ever wondered how rockets fly or how bridges stay up? Math provides the rules and tools to understand how things work, even if we can't see all the parts.

- Mathematical thinking: Math exercises your brain, like running, which strengthens your body. The more you practice, the better you get at solving problems, thinking creatively, and making wise decisions. So, even though math might seem serious sometimes, it's a tool for adventure and discovery! Every time you learn a new math concept, you're unlocking a piece of the puzzle and taking a step closer to understanding the amazing world around you.

- Mathematics is Formal and Abstract: Unlike ordinary, natural languages, math uses mathematical and geometrical symbols, axioms, and rules to express abstract concepts and relationships. It's independent of cultural and specific physical manifestations, aiming for universality and precision.

- The Concepts of Mathematics are Logical and Deductive. Mathematics is built on logic and deduction. We derive new truths from accepted axioms (fundamental truths) through rigorous proofs, creating a self-contained, interconnected web of knowledge.

Mathematics Influences Conscious Awareness

It Sharpens Logic and Reasoning: Learning and using mathematics trains our minds to think logically, identify patterns, and solve problems systematically. This enhances our ability to analyze, reason, and draw valid conclusions in various aspects of life.

Abstract Thought and Mental Models: Mathematics challenges us to grapple with abstract concepts, fostering the development of mental models and frameworks for understanding complex, non-physical ideas. This expands our capacity for abstract thought and imagination.

Understanding the Universe: Mathematics has become a fundamental scientific exploration and discovery tool. It allows us to quantify, model, and analyze the physical world, revealing hidden patterns and unlocking secrets of the universe. This understanding shapes our perception of reality and our place within it.

The language of mathematics has profoundly influenced consciousness. It cultivates logical thinking, expands our capacity for abstract thought, and allows us to grasp the intricacies of the universe. However, it's essential to appreciate its limitations and approach it with a sense of wonder. The interplay between mathematics and consciousness remains an ongoing exploration, offering insights into the human mind and its relationship to the world.

Mathematics is a language within its characterization. Even though mathematical symbols are specific to their definitions, they are still expressed within a semantic context with our natural language to conceptualize their meanings and values. In addition to special characters, math uses numbers and letters to explore and express abstract mathematical concepts and theories. These can be articulated by our natural language we use to communicate and understand our mathematical calculations.

Chapter 8

Verbal Language as a Manipulation Tool

A Branding Tool

Language plays a crucial role in shaping a brand's identity and communicating with its audience. By carefully choosing the words, tone, and communication style, a brand can establish a unique and memorable voice that resonates with its target market. There are many ways in which language can be used as a branding tool.

Tone of Voice

The tone of voice refers to the style and manner in which a brand communicates with its audience. It encompasses the choice of words, sentence structure, and overall attitude conveyed in the brand's messaging. The tone of voice should align with the brand's values, personality, and target audience.

Brand Messaging

Language is used to craft brand messaging that effectively communicates the brand's values, mission, and unique selling points. Consistent and compelling messaging helps differentiate the brand from competitors and creates a strong brand identity.

Content Creation

Language is critical in content creation, including blog posts, social media posts, emails, advertisements, and website copy. The choice of words, storytelling techniques, and overall messaging style contribute to the brand's voice and help engage and connect with the audience.

Brand Storytelling

Language is a powerful tool for brand storytelling. Through storytelling, brands can create emotional connections with their audience, convey their brand's history and values, and engage customers on a deeper level. Using language in storytelling helps shape the brand's narrative and build brand loyalty. Many TV commercials communicate this way through storytelling.

Localization and Translation

Language is essential when expanding a brand's presence into different markets. Localization and translation ensure the brand's messaging is culturally relevant and resonates with the target audience in various regions. Adapting the language to local nuances and preferences helps establish a strong brand presence globally.

Naming and Slogans

Language is used to create brand names and slogans that are memorable, distinctive, and aligned with the brand's identity. A well-crafted brand name and slogan can evoke emotions, communicate the brand's essence, and leave a lasting impression on consumers.

In conclusion, language is a powerful branding tool that helps shape a brand's identity, engage with the audience, and differentiate from competitors. By carefully choosing the tone of voice, crafting compelling messaging, creating engaging content, and adapting to different markets, brands can leverage language to build a solid and memorable brand presence.

Propaganda and its Use of Language

Like branding, propaganda means disseminating information or ideas, often biased or misleading, to influence public opinion and promote a particular cause or agenda. It is typically used in political, social, or ideological contexts.

Language plays a crucial role in propaganda, shaping and manipulating public perception. Propagandists carefully choose their words, phrases, and rhetoric to evoke specific emotions, create a sense of urgency, and persuade the audience to adopt a particular viewpoint. Language in propaganda can distort reality, create a false image, or dehumanize an enemy. By using persuasive language techniques such as loaded words, emotional appeals, and logical fallacies, propagandists aim to sway public opinion in their favor. Fascists and dictators implement these techniques in their speeches. Sound familiar?

Examples of Propaganda's Use of Language

- Dehumanization and Demonization: Propaganda often uses derogatory or racist terms to dehumanize and create hatred towards a supposed enemy. This can be seen in words like racism, fascism, Naziism, communism, socialism, and Marxism, respectively. This is being used in our political narratives in America as we speak.

- Distortion of Reality: Propaganda can distort reality by using language to manipulate facts or present a biased narrative. It may involve making false allegations, avoiding certain words or language, or selectively highlighting information that supports a particular agenda. These techniques are used by the news media all the time.

- Emotional Manipulation: Propaganda frequently employs emotional appeals to evoke strong feelings and sway public opinion. By using language that taps into people's fears, hopes, or desires, propagandists can influence their attitudes and behaviors. Emotional language can create a sense of urgency, rally support, raise money, or demonize opponents.

- Selective Language and Framing: Propaganda often employs selective language and framing techniques to shape public perception. By choosing specific words, phrases, or metaphors, propagandists can influence how an issue is understood and interpreted. This can involve framing an argument favoring a particular viewpoint or using euphemisms to downplay negative aspects.

- Slogans and Catchphrases: Propaganda frequently uses catchy slogans and memorable catchphrases to simplify complex ideas and make them more accessible to the public. These linguistic devices are designed to stick in people's minds and reinforce a particular message or belief. An example is "Make America Great Again."

It is essential to be aware of the language used in propaganda and to evaluate the information presented critically. By understanding the techniques employed, individuals can better recognize and resist the influence of propaganda in shaping public opinion. Authoritative figures in power often use these techniques to either gain more or stay in power. They are misleading and dangerous to a free society.

Gaslighting: A Twisted Use of Language

Gaslighting is a form of psychological manipulation where someone intentionally creates doubt and confusion in another person's mind, making them question their memories, perceptions, and even sanity. This manipulation often relies heavily on language, making it a crucial aspect of understanding and identifying gaslighting behavior.

Here's how language plays a role in gaslighting:

- Denial and contradiction: A gaslighter might flatly deny an event you witnessed, even if you have evidence to the contrary. They might contradict your statements and memories, leaving you questioning your recollection. Take the insurrection of the Capitol in the U.S., which occurred on January 6, 2021. What was televised in plain view was then gaslighted to make people think it was a peaceful tour of the Capitol or that the FBI was responsible. The video shows the truth.

- Trivialization and minimization: Your feelings and concerns are dismissed as overreactions or exaggerations. The gaslighter might make you feel like you're being too sensitive or making a big deal out of nothing.

- Shifting blame: Responsibility for events is deflected onto you, even if the gaslighter was at fault. You might be accused of forgetting, imagining things, or even being crazy.

- Ambiguity and vagueness: The gaslighter might use vague language or double-speak to keep you off balance. They might make indirect comments or leave out crucial information, leaving you to fill in the blanks with your doubts.

- Gaslighting through questioning: Instead of making direct accusations, the gaslighter might ask loaded questions that plant seeds of doubt in your mind. They might question your judgment, memory, or perception of reality, chipping away your confidence.

The Effects of These Language Tactics Can Be Devastating:

- Confusion and self-doubt: You start questioning your memories and perceptions, wondering if you're overreacting or imagining things.

- Loss of confidence: The gaslighter's constant negativity and blame can erode one's self-esteem and make one doubt one's judgment.

- Isolation and dependence: The gaslighter might isolate you from your support system, making you more dependent on them. Example: Stating that opposing news channels are fake news.

- Emotional distress: You might experience anxiety, depression, and even fear as a result of gaslighting.

Recognizing gaslighting through language is crucial:

- Pay attention to your feelings: Do conversations with this person leave you confused, anxious, or insecure?

- Track patterns: Do they consistently use language to undermine your reality?

- Validate your experiences: Talk to trusted friends or family about what's happening. Their perspective can help you see the situation more clearly.

- Seek support: If you're experiencing gaslighting, seeking professional help from a therapist or counselor is essential.

Remember, gaslighting is a form of abuse. It's important to prioritize your well-being and protect yourself from further harm.

Verbal Language in Politics

It's essential to see the political implications of language, as this is an important aspect of contemporary life regarding how we want to live, individually and collectively. Political ideologies have certainly come to the forefront of our societal and educational realities.

In America, political rhetoric has influenced specific populations in this culture, which has had an adverse and detrimental effect on the collective psyche. Authoritative figures that have been in power politically are propagating misinformation deliberately to manipulate people to advocate for their stay in power, even if it takes violence to retain their political positions. They have disfigured our relationships with our institutions and one another. This has been intentionally and consciously done for the benefit of a small minority of people to keep them in power, and it is a power play that undermines the people's will.

Historically, this is not a new pattern or scenario. It has been executed by authoritative figures and dictators from time immemorial. As mentioned, it begins by telling people that certain news and media entities are fake (sound familiar?) or that elections are rigged. Then, a specific population of people begins to believe this or become confused and doubtful when it is repeated over and over again. This is gaslighting!

Those influenced by this misinformation have been manipulated to start watching only the information and news sanctioned and aligned by this political person or group. Thus, a minority group of people become followers of a movement that begins to expand exponentially over time. Unfortunately, this is the current situation that plagues the American people.

Chapter 10: Artificial Intelligence

Chapter 10

Artificial Intelligence

Digital Language and Thought

Artificial Intelligence presents a Digital Language Matrix composed of digital information and content that simulates some characteristics of our verbal language, logic, and conceptual intelligence. It is programmed with language models from volumes of information created and accumulated by humans throughout the ages.

Linguistic models of human thought describe how humans use language to represent and organize their thoughts. Artificial Intelligence (AI) is a digital matrix where machines, software applications, and information programming are compiled to provide specific problem-solving and decision-making computations and predictions. This has created a digital intelligence that is fabricated artificially. There are similarities to how the human mind assimilates, stores, and applies language to affect problem-solving and decision-making conceptually. Digital Language models use algorithms, programming languages, and digital neurotechnology to create and improve digital simulations and calculations.

Artificial "General" Intelligence (AGI) systems can develop their own language matrices, which could be called "The Digital Language Matrix." These matrices are based on the data that the AI systems are trained on, and they can be used to represent and organize the AI's information and knowledge, similarly to how the Human Language Matrix works. AGI systems can be programmed to learn independently and provide required parameters, problem-solving tasks, etc.

The mind has characteristics similar to Artificial General Intelligence (AGI). AGI is artificial Intelligence programmed to learn from its computational and analytic experiences. This aspect of AI is very relevant to problem-solving and exploration. AGI is much more complex and advanced than robotic AI, where only one or two tasks are programmed to be performed repeatedly. On the other hand, AGI can learn from its own computational and analytical experiences. As mentioned, it is also highly creative and imaginative when solving problems. An example of the similarity between AGI and human learning is that, as humans are being educated in school and college, the experience of learning is a conditioning process where information is assimilated and memorized in the mind. Informational knowledge is retained in the subconscious mind as conditioned knowledge. To me, this has similarities to AGI, not that it has consciousness or the complexity of human cognition and sensation. Still, AGI can be programmed to explore and predict specific outcomes within the appropriate parameters to learn and expand on that particular information or knowledge it is provided with. AGI is a reality and is being explored by scientists as we speak.

Artificial General Intelligence (AGI) is rapidly developing the ability to process and understand our verbal language. These matrices are similar to the Human Language Matrix in many ways. They are both complex systems of interconnected concepts, ideas, and relationships. However, there are also some critical differences. One of the key differences is that Digital Language Matrices are much more explicit than the Human Language Matrices. This is because AI systems can explicitly represent concepts and relationships in ways humans cannot. This allows AI systems to develop and learn in a much more systematic way. Another key difference is that Digital Language Matrices are much more flexible than the Human Language Matrix. AGI systems can dynamically create and modify their matrices as they learn and experience new things. AGI systems can adapt to new situations and learn more quickly than humans.

Despite these differences, Digital Language Matrices are becoming increasingly similar to the Human Language Matrix. AI systems are learning to understand and use language like humans do. As AI systems continue to develop, the similarities between the two systems will likely continue to grow. Here are some of the similarities between Human Language Matrices and Digital Language Matrices:

- Both types of matrices are based on language models. Language is a powerful tool for representing and organizing complex thoughts and ideas.
- Both types of matrices are dynamic and constantly evolving. Our Human Language Matrix evolves accordingly as humans learn and experience new things. Similarly, as AI systems are trained on

new data, their Digital Language Matrices also evolve.

- Both types of matrices can generate new thoughts and ideas. Humans use their Language Matrix to develop new ideas, solve problems, and create new works of art and literature. Similarly, AI systems can use their digital language matrices to generate new creative text formats, translate languages, and write creative content.

Here are some specific examples of how AI systems are using language to create digital language matrices as digital thought:

- Large language models (LLMs), such as GPT-4, Bard, Gemini, and Bing, are being trained on massive datasets of text and code. This allows them to predict language probabilities accurately and use them to represent and organize information. LLMs can then use this knowledge to generate new text, translate languages, and answer questions comprehensively and informally based on probability and predictability factors.

- Knowledge graphs are another way of representing and organizing information in a digital format. They comprise nodes and edges, where nodes represent entities and edges represent relationships between entities. AI systems can use knowledge graphs to store and retrieve information, reason about and make inferences from that information, and more.

Knowledge graphs have some technical correlation to the human subconscious mind in that they are hidden data storage and can store information and create a network of conceptual digital neuro-links to provide comprehensive data retrieval.

- Semantic networks are similar to knowledge graphs, but they focus on representing the meaning of words and phrases. Semantic networks can improve the performance of AI systems in tasks such as natural language processing and machine translation.

As AGI technology develops, we expect to see even more sophisticated and powerful Digital Language Matrices. These matrices will allow AGI systems to appear to think and reason digitally, more like humans, and enable us to interact with AI systems more naturally and intuitively.

The correlation between AI and Human language and intelligence is that both systems can arrive at the same conclusions even though digital AI uses predictive computations and computational information analysis. Humans are not that systematic, and many factors, such as sensory information, stored conceptual information, and creative imagination, determine the differences between the digital and human experience. There exist some erroneous outcomes of information derived by AI that are termed "hallucinations." These discrepancies in digital knowledge accuracy are being refined and corrected as the industry progresses.

There are some essential differences between the two systems:

- The human Language Matrix is implicit, while Digital Language Matrices are explicit.
- The human Language Matrix is relatively static, while Digital Language Matrices are dynamic.
- The human Language Matrix is grounded in our physical experience of the world, while Digital Language Matrices are not.

Despite these differences, the similarities between the Human Language Matrices and Digital Language Matrices of digital thought are striking. As AI systems continue developing, they will likely become increasingly similar.

The Digital Language Matrices have the potential to revolutionize the way we think and interact with the world around us. For example, AI systems could be used to:

- Develop new scientific theories and discoveries.
- Create new forms of art and entertainment.
- Help us to understand ourselves and the world around us better.
- Solve complex social and environmental problems.

As AI systems continue to develop, it is essential to consider how to use them to benefit humanity. We must ensure that AI systems align with our values and are used responsibly and ethically.

Chapter 11: Conceptual Realization

Chapter 11

Conceptual Realization

Conceptual Realization as it Relates to Self-Realization

I've understood that most spiritual seekers are compulsive, needing to read and study books and scriptures. They attend discourses on spiritual topics and view videos and documentaries on spirituality. They need to understand their relative existence and gain a spiritual understanding of their metaphysical existence conceptually to fulfill the mind's desire for knowledge and curiosity.

When conceived conceptually, insights, discoveries, and revelations provide the mind's fuel and energy for an aspirant to stay committed to self-inquiry and discovery. Intellectually, this path involves acquiring conceptual knowledge as the search proceeds. This experience is necessary for most and seems inevitable for those seeking Self-realization or enlightenment. Initially, one needs an intellectual frame of reference to guide one forward and the ego provides this entanglement, as it says, "Let me help you with this." This is how a spiritual seeker is born.

Pursuing the truth can be conceived through the use of language. However, language hides the truth from the conscious view by conceptualizing a fabricated reality in one's mind that the ego identifies as real. It is our false egoic mind that is seeking to know what is real. In this pursuit, the ego attempts over and over again to become awakened, and these attempts eventually become futile and exhaust the mind's efforts. The ego, the egoic mind, is trying to figure all this out and enlighten itself. It can only attempt this by conceptualizing the pursuit by reading books and scriptures, attending discourses, and practicing spiritual disciplines. This type of behavior is what the human egoic mind does. It provides a frame of reference and a pathway to follow in a disciplined practice of spirituality. However, the ego will never attain an enlightened state because enlightenment is beyond the ego and any conceptual understanding.

If this sounds familiar, you may have begun to experience a dispassion or detachment from conceptual thinking. You start to see the irrelevance of your mind's unsuccessful attempts to enlighten itself. You may undergo a frustrating experience that you can only resolve by surrendering your pursuit because you begin to see the futility of continuing it. At this point, the door to awakening opens, giving you a glimpse of who you are non-conceptually. The presence of silent witnessing and observing reveals the true Self when the ego relinquishes its autonomy and subsides.

All efforts to comprehend the human experience or worldly experience are transcended, and a unified field of oneness or wholeness is experienced, and it is evident that it has always been there. Once empty awareness sees itself as the silent self, the egoic self submits to its descent of power, and over time, the ego dissolves naturally without effort. When the truth is seen, that which is untrue vanishes; when a light is brought into the darkness, the darkness disappears.

Self-realization happens when a person emerges from a dream-like existence of false fabrications of an imagined reality. This awakened state of cognition knows itself as an unknowable and incomprehensible presence that is fundamental and Absolute. This is the essence of how a conceptual realization is a jumping-off point for transcending subjective and objective reality.

The content of this book originated from the intellectual experience I've acquired in my path. The educational topics I've assimilated into my mind's knowledge and the many occupational and spiritual practices I've had have inspired me to understand this information and knowledge. The knowledge in this book explains why we all have this human experience related to our verbal and nonverbal reality.

Mistaking Conceptual Realization as Your True Self

Mistaking conceptual realization for true self-realization is the most detrimental spiritual condition. It obstructs, hides, and prevents the true Self from being realized. There are a lot of people professing to be awakened. It is only partially true if someone tells you they have awakened. Their conceptual realization provides them with conceptual information that validates their claim by what they know conceptually and communicate. This may happen when one has had many spiritual experiences, insights, and epiphanies. One begins to think that they have awakened and now know what's real and what's not. One starts to believe that there's nothing more to seek or understand. They finally got it! This entrapment is another attachment to conceptual thinking that you must awaken to. It doesn't reveal the true Self; the spiritual ego identifies itself as awakened. Subjectively, this is another egoic identification that creates another veil of ignorance that falls upon pure awareness and hides the true Self.

You must remember that the true Self is Absolute and is "beyond your mind" or ego's intellectual comprehension. The egoic mind cannot realize the true Self. There's nothing more to say about this. Only the cognizance of the true Self cognizes itself in silence, stillness, and beyond the concepts of enlightenment or illusive entanglements. It cannot be fabricated!

There is no person there to experience a Self. You are that one Self that experiences itself as a nonconceptual being. It is beyond existence and non-existence. It only knows itself! You are That!

NON-VERBAL REALITY

PART TWO

Non-Verbal Reality

Introduction

The idea of a Non-verbal reality occurs when conceptual thinking is subsided and mental fabrications are silenced in the mind. Once one becomes aware of this silence, it renders its presence as the underlying consciousness expressing the present moment and all that appears "as it is" unfabricated and unconditioned.

The experience of a non-verbal reality is not what an ordinary person would consider a possibility. The thinking mind appears to be the only intellectual experience available. In this case, the mind is always focused outwardly, experiencing appearances and disappearances as if real. This is called ignorance, in that one is ignoring what is true for that which is untrue. What appears and disappears in our awareness is defined and characterized by a conceptual thought process artificially fabricated by our use of language.

Without this conceptualization, it has no substantial existence other than a conceptual one manufactured by the mind.

What happens when your mind stops thinking, and you are silently experiencing what is appearing without any thought about it? Is that even possible? Everyone has had moments when the mind is not thinking, and everything becomes calm and quiet. Some may have experienced a pervading peace and contentment that created a perfect experience of harmony without the thinking mind chattering in the background. With a nonconceptual mind, there's nothing to do or to be within a conceptual context. Everything is neither perfect nor imperfect. It's just what it is.

In the present moment, the presence of being yourself is experiencing the emptiness of no thought with an empty mind. You can be happy and contented without conceptualizing your reality; there's nothing to do or to be conceptually, and the empty mind provides an effortless experience of your true Self that underlies all appearances in your awareness. This emptiness reveals a unified and fundamental reality that emerges as the presence of one's true being when the conceptual ego is absent. This view is apart from any physical or mental experience. It is an unknowable clarity that a conceptualized mind cannot comprehend. You can only be this; you can't "think" or conceptualize the Absolute into an intellectualized being.

It is difficult to comprehend or describe a nonverbal reality as it is not defined within a language-based frame of reference. Without thoughts or conceptualization, it is entirely non-dualistic. Without a past and future, it takes on an unknown context indescribable by any mental description that can be expressed through words.

What if nothing is labeled, categorized, or intellectually conceived by language or verbal thought? What if the mind is empty of thoughts? In this instance, a silent "be-ness" is fundamental awareness observing appearances and disappearances arising in the conscious mind. When nothing is labeled or categorized by language, appearances in the mind's awareness are perceived precisely "as they are" without verbal commentary. This reality emerges from a silent mind, where no conceptualization or rationalized behavior exists. It is not a phenomenal experience in space and time, as these concepts do not exist in this realm.

You might think a silent, empty mind is useless in our physical and mental environments. Objective reality, as mentioned previously, still appears as a physical phenomenon. Subjective reality takes on a different face when not conceptualized by language. It is an empirical experience where emotions and feelings are sensed but not rationalized. They are experienced within a silent space where attention is not focused on thoughts about them. They are not conceived conceptually by verbal thinking. Subjective and objective reality are experienced precisely as they appear without verbal attributes. This is pure naked awareness, unconditioned. This unconditioned view frees one from the entrapments of conditioned conceptualizations. It provides a neutral environment to engage and participate without assumptions or presumptions that limit one's experience of reality.

Consciousness is Absolute and beyond body and mind. It has always been present and will continue to be, with or without a body. Concepts of birth and death do not exist. These are merely extreme conceptual ideas fabricated by the mind and are untrue.

As you can see, this is a very challenging realm to explore and attempt to explain. It has paradoxical implications: A relative reality exists conceptually, and an Absolute reality exists that transcends dualistic concepts of existence and nonexistence. As we proceed in this discourse, my use of language may appear paradoxical in this attempt. However, an expanded view is experienced when a conceptual reality is realized to be falsely fabricated or misrepresented, and then it becomes apparent what the mind is and is not.

Chapter 12

Energy, Vibration, and Frequency

Energy is often described as the ability to do work. It's an essential part of everything around us, from tiny atoms bouncing around to the vast movements of galaxies. Understanding energy helps us explain how the world works and how we can utilize it for various purposes.

Energy as a Fundamental Concept in Physics

Consider how we could experience our physical and mental environments energetically. Imagine that our experiences can be felt as a field of energy vibrating in specific vibrations and frequencies. And the Universe emerges from these energies by the frequencies of their vibrations. Every particle and wave is vibrating at frequencies that are unique to each. These vibrations manifest when consciousness becomes concentrated into specific vibrational patterns that produce one or multiple forms. These manifestations exist as physical matter or thoughts, as they are subtle or gross manifestations.

These dynamically create our physical and mental worlds as the stream of consciousness creates, sustains, and destroys. This could be similar to the quantum field, where existential manifestations are created and transformed fundamentally.

What is Energy?

- Energy exists in various forms, including kinetic, potential, thermal, electrical, chemical, and nuclear.

- Energy can be converted from one form to another. However, the law of conservation of energy states that energy cannot be created or destroyed, only transformed. Thus, the total amount of energy in a closed system remains constant.

Apparent "creation" and "destruction" can often be explained as a transfer of energy in and out of a system. For example, a nuclear power plant creates energy. Still, it converts the potential energy stored in nuclear material into electrical and thermal energy while releasing some as radiation into the environment.

Therefore, it's crucial to distinguish between true energy creation and destruction and its transformation or transfer from one form to another. These concepts form the foundation of our understanding of energy in the universe.

The Correlation of Consciousness and Energy May Be Similar

Consciousness is the fundamental source of existence and creation. It is a constant in the same manner that energy is. It cannot be created or destroyed and can only be transformed into subtle and gross forms. Consciousness is the source of the creative and destructive energies of the universe, which is the ground of existence itself. To understand this, it is like the metaphor I used regarding the ocean and the waves of the ocean: The sea is analogous to consciousness that, on the surface, takes the form of waves. The waves appear and dissolve by the conditions of the ocean. The ocean and the waves cannot be separated. All is ocean.

Consciousness takes form as the physical and mental manifestations of subjective and objective reality. The correlation between consciousness and energy is similar to the law of energy conservation, i.e., energy cannot be created or destroyed; it can only be transformed. Consciousness functions similarly and manifests in multiple forms, as its appearance resembles a realistic dream.

Is Mental Activity An Energy of Thought Creation?

Thought is an internal process involving perception, memory, reasoning, and imagination. It's associated with electrical activity in the brain, particularly the cerebral cortex. While the exact link between brain activity and thought remains a mystery, neuroscientists continue to unravel how neurons, neurotransmitters, and brain networks contribute to our cognitive processes. The brain isn't just a lump of tissue; it's a highly metabolic organ requiring a sustained energy supply (around 20% of the body's total energy use).

Neural activity, including neurons firing and transmitting signals, consumes energy in glucose and oxygen. Different patterns of brain activity likely correspond to other types of thoughts. For example, increased activity in the visual cortex may indicate visual imagery, while increased activity in the prefrontal cortex may indicate complex reasoning.

However, how energy directly "becomes" thought remains unanswered. Some propose that specific arrangements of neurons and their firing patterns could encode particular thoughts, but a comprehensive theory is yet to be established. Other schools of thought explore the relationship between consciousness and energy in more philosophical or spiritual frameworks. Is thought energy a linguistic process where language processing is an energetic form that creates the conceptual mind?

Some spiritual and philosophical traditions associate thought with subtle energy fields or consciousness, proposing a nonphysical dimension beyond conventional physics. The concept of mind/body dualism, which separates the mind and body as distinct entities, further complicates understanding how energy relates to thought. Ultimately, how energy manifests as thought remains a vibrant frontier of scientific and philosophical inquiry, with much room for exploration and discovery.

Is it possible that thoughts abide inside and outside the body and mind, residing in individual and collective mental fields of energy providing the source for all conceptual thinking? Could these be a mental grid or a conceptual field of thought content that the mind can tune into and fabricate conceptual realities? Is this field the source of thought creation with all the potential to create verbal conceptualization? It may be similar to a mental or intellectual field of quantum energy where all possibilities can manifest as thoughts inspired by the conditioning of the conscious and subconscious mind.

The brain is much like a receiver and transmitter, capable of connecting to these mental environments. The brain can tune in to specific thoughts, emotions, or feelings stored in this mental field, similar to how a radio is tuned to a particular station. Each frequency is a radio station or a channel of our mind that, when focused by a specific frequency, creates reality paradigms fabricated by conceptualized thoughts to develop a dominant model, framework, or way of thinking about something. The conscious and subconscious mind have a direct connection to this information. This may explain or clarify some confusion about how thoughts are created and applied to a reality matrix, conceptually.

Overall, while energy manifesting as thought is intuitive and captivating, the scientific understanding of the precise link is still evolving. Researchers continue to investigate the complex interplay between brain activity, energy metabolism, and the generation of our inner world of thoughts and experiences.

Vibrations and Frequencies

Everything in the universe is vibrating and is in motion. Nothing in the physical or mental world is devoid of vibration and frequency. These vibrations vibrate at specific frequencies that provide the conditions for everything to exist in many forms, from the atomic level to the gross physical world. These vibrations emerge as sound and light; everything vibrates as light or sound waves, each in distinct and specific frequencies. Even thoughts are formed by the vibration of mental energy, creating concrete appearances in our minds as images or concepts of thought. They are forms of energy, and as mentioned, our mind is tuned to the frequencies of these energies, similar to tuning a radio to a particular station.

The concept of manifestation occurs when the mind is matched to the same frequency as what it desires or is trying to create. The brain is like a radio receiver and transmitter aligned to vibrations and frequencies that appear and disappear in awareness. When the mind's vibrational frequency is tuned to the same frequency as what it wants to create, it can create subjects or objects.

Here's an example: If you want to buy a new car, you begin by researching and tuning your awareness to many types of vehicles. When you find a car that "resonates" vibrationally with your physical and aesthetic requirements, you have narrowed your search to a specific possibility. Your mind is attuned to one car that meets all of your needs. Then, correspondingly, matching your frequency to the object's frequency enables it to manifest in your reality. This is possible, especially when these frequencies establish emotions and feelings that solidify the potential for the desired manifestation. Persistent intention and focusing on the result as if it has already happened create the fulfillment of our desires. This is an example of how vibrations and frequencies create our realities.

MIKE MARINELLI

Equanimity of Energies
by Michael Murphy Burke

The Equinox is like a reckoning

A beautiful evenness of day and night

An Equanimity of energies

A cosmic dance of Divine Delight

There's a spaciousness that permeates

And caresses the Symmetry within

We are guided to balance our Darkness

With the Light that we bring in

We are the letters of the words

That write the poems that we all know

We are the Rhymes that Tickle Souls

From this Blessed Ebb and Flow

So, on this Sacred Day, my friends

Be at One with who You are

You are the Essence

Of all the Light from every Star

Yes, there is Light in every Shadow

And every Shadow shapes our Light

We Balance upon this Equinox

Holy Day with Hallowed Night.

Dancing with the Shadows, Michael Burke - 2023 "Equinimity of Energies" Pages 100-101 Mountain Arbor Press, Alpharetta, GA

Chapter 12: Non-Verbal Language in Art

Chapter 12

Non-Verbal Language in Art

Music is a Language Produced by the Vibrations of Sound

Music is produced by vibrating the air with specialized instruments to create sound vibrations of one or more pitches. Sound can provide a structured presentation of musical ideas if organized and structured into cohesive and logical expressive patterns, melodically and rhythmically. Depending on whether the music is instrumental or vocal, these musical ideas can be either a verbal or nonverbal experience perceived by the ear.

Nonverbal Visual Art

An artist paints a depiction of a nature scene that he is directly experiencing in the present moment. He might also envision an imaginative landscape and create these mental images on the canvas. These depictions of real or imagined images are nonverbal experiences painted on the canvas. However, the subjective interpretations of the observer's experiences are conditioned by verbal language, conceptual association, and subjective biases.

Nature and Environmental Sounds

We are perceptive to sound continuously. The sounds of nature, the sound of traffic, the sounds of a crowd of people, etc. These are spontaneous sounds that are created in our environments naturally. We don't think of these sounds as music, although some would perceive the sound of a flowing stream as a musical sound of nature. Sound landscapes continuously surround us with their spontaneous pulsations and creative constructs. Everything in the Universe vibrates and thus creates a sound. Even your body is creating a specific sound and frequency. Most of us block out these as they are irrelevant to our experience of the present moment.

Other Forms of Nonverbal Art

The performing and visual arts can be contextualized in the same way that music is a symbolic expression of the human experience. Each expresses its art forms in specific ways that communicate and integrate mental and physical imagery, an essential aspect of human expression, development, and evolution.

The acquisition and development of skills required to manifest works of art are inspired by language to communicate all conceptual aspects of the educational process. Highly skilled artists will transcend technical skills and even forgo preconceived ideas or concepts to create artwork, sometimes called improvisational or "out of the box." Whether using sound or visual expressions, these art forms are unique creations formed by the artist that are considered original works of art.

Chapter 13: Eastern and Western Religions

Chapter 13

Eastern and Western Religions

Religions and Spiritual Scriptures

Religions and their spiritual scriptures are essential aspects that have impacted human behavior and influenced societies immensely. The various schools of religion, philosophy, etc., utilize conceptual thinking through language, creating mental conditions for religious practices to inspire and provide spiritual understanding.

Spiritual scriptures provide the guidelines and conceptual understanding of many spiritual practices. Spiritual scriptures exist in every religion. They are the insights and expressions of the masters or the creators of each religion. These insights and practices expound the beliefs or principles of their faith. In many ways, the spiritual insights of their founders and the application of their spiritual practices have become ritualistic over time. Scriptures provide pathways to understanding the spiritual journey as viewed by the specific religion, language, and timeframe. Most have a common morality and an ethical thread in their discourses.

Spiritual scriptures and discourses have created matrices of abstract thinking that have influenced humans since the beginning. Even though spiritual and mystical experiences may be empirical and intuitive, their verbal expressions are immersed in conceptual thinking as the primary source for creating and communicating a religious human experience.

Spiritual scriptures, books, and videos should be viewed as tools only. These resources may quicken one's conceptual realization as they increase spiritual awareness. And the seeds of spiritual practice are planted to eventually lead one to surrendering and letting go of the ego identification.

Eastern Religion

"Eastern Religion" encompasses a vast and diverse array of belief systems originating in East, South, and Southeast Asia. Here are some of the most prominent examples that I'm familiar with, along with summaries of their core doctrines:

Hinduism: The world's oldest religion, characterized by a belief in one supreme reality (Brahman or God) that manifests in countless forms, including various deities (like Brahma, Vishnu, and Shiva - the creator, sustainer, and destroyer). It emphasizes concepts like dharma (righteousness), karma (action and consequence), and moksha (liberation from the conditioned mind).

Buddhism: Founded by Siddhartha Gautama, Buddhism revolves around self-realization and enlightenment (nirvana) through meditation, the Four Noble Truths, and the Eightfold Path. It emphasizes non-violence, compassion, mindfulness, and detachment from worldly desires. Zen Buddhism is the most modern form of Buddhism.

Most Eastern religions conceive of a view of God as being the only thing that exists. If so, everything that appears is subjectively or objectively that of God alone. One God and not anything else! This is a nondualistic and transcendental view of religion or reality shared by Eastern cultures.

Western Religions

The term "Western religions" can be somewhat ambiguous, as people may have slightly different understandings of what it encompasses. Abrahamic religions often refer to the three

Abrahamic religions: Judaism, Christianity, and Islam. These religions share a common origin in the Hebrew Bible and belief in one God, Yahweh/Allah. They have significantly impacted Western culture, history, and philosophy.

Focusing on the values and practices often associated with Western culture, such as individualism, secularism, and an emphasis on human reason, has influenced many cultures.

The Concept of Sin in Religion

"Sin" is a complex concept with varying interpretations across cultures and religious traditions. It has impacted our societies intellectually and emotionally through the mental constructs of language and conceptual thinking. Many concepts that describe sin are fabrications of manipulative efforts to convince people of or convert them to a religion.

In many religions, sin is viewed as a violation of God's laws or principles. Sin can encompass actions, thoughts, or even inaction. Specific religious texts, like the Ten Commandments in the Abrahamic traditions, often outline what constitutes sin.

Sin can also be thought of as the idea that ignorance prevails and separates man from God. Man became self-conscious as a separate agent apart from God by the egoic identities created in his mind, and this sin threw him out of the heavenly state of the Absolute.

Sin can also be seen as a barrier between humans and the divine, disrupting the relationship. Reconciliation with the divine may require atonement or forgiveness through specific rituals or practices.

Beyond specific religious laws, sin can also represent a broader concept of moral wrongdoings, such as harming others, acting selfishly or dishonestly, or violating basic ethical principles.

In a non-religious context, even outside of religious frameworks, the term "sin" can describe actions that are considered wrong or harmful, either to oneself or others. These can include lying, cheating, stealing, or engaging in destructive behaviors, which may have legal consequences.

A more individualistic view sees sin as internal conflict or dissonance between one's values and actions. This could involve acting against one's conscience, betraying personal beliefs, or succumbing to temptations one deems harmful.

These ideas are conceptual and have spurred many interpretations. They are conceptual fabrications using spiritual language to rationalize one's religious beliefs. Some religious ideologies proselytize the concept that man and God may be co-creators.

Is the Idea of Co-Creation a Fabrication?

Co-creation in a religious context is a belief that humans are not passive recipients of God's grace but active participants in the ongoing creation and unfolding of reality. It emphasizes the importance of human agency, responsibility, and spiritual growth within the context of a divine plan.

The word co-creator reflects the freedom of humans to participate in fulfilling God's purposes (a view sometimes criticized for super-elevating humans to the same level as God)

The co-creation idea is a fabricated conceptual agreement that says God provides the energy potential that allows man to manifest those potentials into actuality. Because of this co-dependency and transactional experience between God and the human imagination of the mind, it is thought that God provides the source, and man steers the ship to fulfill God's purpose through one's free will. This relationship creates the idea of Co-Creation. It is a concept that together, they occupy creative roles that manifest realities and spiritual experiences. Co-creation emphasizes the importance of human agency, responsibility, and spiritual growth within a divine plan.

So, I must ask, "Does language and conditioning have anything to do with conceiving the idea of the Co-Creator and adopting an agreement such as Co-Creation?" Co-creation is a concept and a way of thinking within a verbal context to justify a working relationship between God and man.

Some Western Religious Ideologies and Practices

Some Western religions, particularly Protestant religions, have developed based on the "fear of God" to manipulate their congregants to be good and have pure moral and ethical aspirations. Many doctrines and laws had a religious and political agenda to rule the masses by advocating moral and ethical standards by the Church as the ruling factor. Some religions that want to rule politically have agendas that incorporate their rhetoric to influence cultures by gaslighting a religious matrix to benefit governments, such as what we are experiencing currently in the USA. In the U.S., a minority group of

Christian Nationalists and White Supremacists have become political and joined a cult that worships one authoritative person. Their goal is to destroy the democratic government that most of the people want to sustain.

To Summarize, Let's face it: religions are conceptual, and their messages and expressions are created through language. The creation of religions uses word meanings as a construct to conceive and communicate moral and ethical values, judgemental expectations, religious ideologies, and religious laws. The sound of the word "God" has an assigned word meaning that could be different from one religion to the next. We understand religion by what it says, what it means, and what it stands for.

Chapter 14: Metaphysics – Mysticism – Spirituality

Chapter 14

Metaphysics, Mysticism, and Spirituality

Metaphysics

Metaphysics is a vast and fascinating philosophical field; its definition can be complicated. At its core, metaphysics delves into the most fundamental questions about the nature of reality itself. It asks questions like, "What is?" and "How is it?" broadly and abstractly. This includes exploring concepts like:

- Existence and being: What does it mean for something to exist? Are there different types of existence?

- Identity and change: How do things stay the same while also changing over time? What defines the identity of a thing?

- Space and time: Are space and time fundamental features of reality, or are they constructs of our minds?

- Cause and effect: What is the nature of causality? Is it a necessary and universal principle, or are there exceptions?

- Consciousness and mind: What is consciousness? How does it relate to the physical brain? Does it exist independently?

While science investigates the physical world through observation and experimentation, metaphysics goes beyond this realm. It explores questions about nonphysical entities like souls, God, and other dimensions of existence.

Throughout history, philosophers have employed various methods to tackle metaphysical questions. These include:

- A priori reasoning: Using logic and deduction to derive conclusions about the nature of reality from basic principles.

- Empirical investigation: Examining our experiences and intuitions to gain insights into the nature of reality.

- Thought experiments: Hypothetical scenarios designed to explore the implications of different metaphysical ideas.

Is it science or philosophy? This is a debated topic. Some argue that metaphysics is bad science, as it can't be tested empirically. Others distinguish it as a distinct kind of inquiry, concerned with questions that lie beyond the reach of science or conceptual thinking.

Why is it important? Metaphysics may not provide definitive answers, but it raises crucial questions about our place in the universe and the meaning of life. Engaging with these questions can deepen our understanding of ourselves and the world around us, even if we never reach a final resolution. Ultimately, exploring metaphysics is an ongoing quest to grapple with the mysteries of existence. It's a journey of intellectual curiosity and a call to contemplate the fundamental nature of reality itself.

Mysticism

Mysticism delves into the realm of direct experience of ultimate reality or truth. It is not easily defined, encompassing various practices and traditions across multiple cultures and religions. However, here are some critical aspects of mysticism:

- Direct experience: Unlike intellectual or religious teachings, mysticism emphasizes a personal, immediate experience of the divine, the Absolute, or a deeper understanding of reality. This experience can be felt, intuited, or even ineffable, defying language and categorization.

- Union or Oneness: Many mystics describe a connection or complete union with the ultimate reality. This can involve transcending individual limitations and ego, feeling deeply interconnected with all things, or experiencing a loss of separateness from the divine.

- Altered states of consciousness: While not an essential element of all mystical traditions, some mystics report experiencing altered states of consciousness during their journeys. These states can involve deep meditation, ecstatic insights, or visionary experiences that provide new insights or perspectives on reality.

- Transformation and transcendence: At its core, mysticism often leads to a profound transformation of the individual. Through their experiences, mystics may develop a heightened sense of compassion, a deeper understanding of themselves and the world, and a commitment to living by spiritual or universal truths.

- Diverse expressions: Mystical traditions and practices vary greatly across cultures and periods. Examples include Christian mysticism, Sufi mysticism, Jewish Kabbalah, Hindu Bhakti and Vedantism, Buddhist meditation practices, and various indigenous spiritual traditions. Each tradition brings unique approaches and interpretations to pursue direct spiritual experience.

Mysticism isn't without its challenges. The subjective nature of the experiences can make them difficult to verify or communicate, leading to skepticism and misconceptions. However, for many, the potential for profound transformation and connection to something greater than oneself makes mysticism a compelling and enduring pursuit. Suppose you're interested in exploring mysticism further. In that case, look into specific traditions that resonate with you, read the works of mystics and scholars, or engage in practices like meditation or contemplation that can open the doors to your inner depths.

Remember, there's no single right way to approach mysticism. It's a personal journey of exploration and discovery, and what matters most is your genuine curiosity and openness to the possibilities of spiritual experience and understanding.

Esoteric Religions and Spirituality

Pure religions have always had an esoteric element that only a few devoted practitioners and ascetics have aligned themselves with. Their metaphysical doctrines and practices are empirical instead of conceptual. Here, there is a metaphysical application of spiritual identity and practices similar to Eastern spirituality, where the concept of God is experienced as one's "True Self." This is not a personal view or an egotistical identification. It is a transcendental, mystical experience of knowing and being free of a conceptual language or an ideological matrix. It is a silent knowledge of the presence of God within one's self as consciousness itself. This may be equated to all creation as being "in the image of God" or "as the presence of God." Thus, there is no separation of subject and object. All is one, and one is all. I think this is the view of the Christian mystics, similar to many Eastern mystics.

Chapter 15: Suspending Conceptual Thinking

Chapter 15

Suspending Conceptual Thinking

Silencing the Mind

What if you hit the mute button in your mind, and language and conceptual thinking were suspended or turned off? Without language, your mind could not define, describe, analyze, or discriminate anything in the usual way. You would be utterly alone in your mind without even a concept of yourself as a person. You would be without any reference to something that exists or does not exist, as these would only be further concepts of thought. You would be completely alone, and "there would only be one in the room," so to speak. There would be no subjects or objects. This experience would be like traversing a journey from the "alone to the alone." Many of us dislike being alone. But this aloneness is not loneliness. Here, you're not depending on any physical or mental object to keep you company. And you don't have to have anything or remove anything to make yourself happy or whole. You are not codependently bound to anything. You are pure and empty awareness that is not colored or conditioned by the conceptual mind. Here, your mind is empty of conceptual thought, and all appearances are experienced "as they are" out of space and time. Space and time are concepts. All appearances spontaneously come and go in your awareness as cognition and perception allow.

I see that consciousness and Absolute reality exist outside of space and time. Space and time are abstract ideas conceived to create and express measurements and dimensions. However, these cause a contraction of consciousness to conform to these conditions. The Absolute, as consciousness, is a spontaneous experience of a perpetual presence of emptiness that streams endlessly.

The present moment has no past or future, as these are only concepts. Conscious awareness is immediate, and its presence is known and felt intuitively and instinctively when thoughts have subsided.

Try doing this: Stop thinking with your mind. Don't associate yourself with any thought. (This is more difficult than you can imagine.) If I say,

"Don't think of a red elephant," in your mind, most people will not be able to stop thinking of a red elephant. So, don't try to stop thoughts from appearing; just observe them silently. Don't grab onto any thought that appears in your mind. Ask yourself, "Who is the thinker of this thought?" The thought will disappear when you don't have a conceptual answer to this question, and silence will permeate your awareness. So, whenever a thought appears, ask, "Who is the thinker of this thought?" Don't provide an answer; just look and see what's there when you are not "thinking."

Settle into your silence, relax into your awareness, and see what's there when you are not conceptualizing thoughts as they appear. Do you disappear when you are not thinking? When you are thinking, who's the thinker? Don't conceptualize an answer with a verbal response; just observe and experience a thoughtless answer. Is there a silent perception that is free of conceptual fabrication or imagination?

In this state, can you remain quiet and see multiple experiences of subjective and objective manifestations emerging in awareness, physically and mentally? These perceptions don't require conceptual thought or definition. Without using language to define and describe all that appears or disappears, there is a silent presence underlying all appearances, and it is just one whole thing, not two. Our language, ego identities, and beliefs separate us from everything and make us feel like subjects and objects are appearing in our awareness.

The unifying principle is the silent awareness when conceptual thinking is suspended or transcended. There is only oneness that can be equated to pure, unconditional consciousness. This is not to be sought for or conceived of in any fashion because it already exists in each person, individually and collectively. You could say that all of this is the image of God manifested in form just like waves appearing in the ocean.

Chapter 16

Consciousness and Awareness

What is Consciousness?

This question has been the most puzzling, and many scientists have been obsessed with finding an answer throughout the ages. It has often been called "the hard problem."

Consciousness cannot be understood because it is the indefinable and fundamental source that enables all manifestations to come into being. It is an incomprehensible entity that is not perceptible to our physical senses. In other words, it's not a fabrication or an imagined concept that the body or mind can comprehend. It is not a subject or object that can be perceived, just as the eyes cannot see themselves. Consciousness is beyond conceptual or dualistic thinking.

If consciousness is beyond what language can express or define, it would be related to nothingness by all logical reasoning. If everything comes from nothing and the idea of nothing can't be understood by a conceptual understanding, it can't be defined or imagined by the mind. Also, it cannot be comprehended as a concept of the mind, as nothing means "no thing." Comprehension doesn't exist in this context. Try to think of nothing existing. If nothing exists, you can't exist either, and so you can't exist to see that nothing exists.

Consciousness itself is not local to any one agent. It is a universal source of all phenomena that is expressed through as many agents or objects that exist. As mentioned, consciousness and Absolute reality exist outside of space and time. Space and time are abstract ideas conceived to create and express measurements and dimensions. However, these cause a contraction of consciousness to conform to these conditions. The Absolute, as consciousness, is a spontaneous experience of a perpetual presence of emptiness that streams endlessly. The present moment has no past or future, as these are only concepts. Conscious awareness is immediate, and its presence is known and felt intuitively and instinctively when thoughts have subsided.

As Carl Jung stated, consciousness exists in humanity's collective experience within the collective unconscious realm. However, it goes beyond that. Consciousness is not an entity that can be imagined or understood intellectually; it is incomprehensible to the thinking mind. In any case, language cannot explain or define what consciousness is and will probably not be able to do so. Consciousness is empty awareness itself, and it is empty of any conceptual content. Awareness is a quality of consciousness that allows one to experience subjective and objective appearances. But consciousness itself is not a subject or an object. It is beyond that and, therefore, cannot be understood by the mind.

The law of energy conservation states that energy cannot be created or destroyed, only transformed. The total amount of power in a closed system remains constant. This is similar to consciousness in that consciousness cannot be created or destroyed and is a continuous and perpetual field beyond existence and nonexistence. It can be transformed into unlimited physical and mental appearances that comprise everything in the universe. In other words, God-energy (consciousness) may manifest expressions of its creative existence as psychological and physical forms. These forms are not sustainable by any authentic substance other than a conceptual one. As mentioned previously, consciousness and energy have a correlation and a similarity, which is the fabric of the appearances of relative phenomena.

Can Language Define Consciousness?

A definition of consciousness has been proposed that refers to it as a state of being aware of having experiences subjectively through one's thoughts, feelings, and perceptions and also by having a sense of self-awareness or self-consciousness. These definitions fall short of depicting what consciousness is other than a purely conceptual definition that doesn't provide a substantial existence.

Creating a definition of consciousness is the most challenging. Philosophers and scientists grapple with this continuously. Psychologists like Stuart Sutherland express his skepticism about defining what it is in his book, "The Macmillan Dictionary of Psychology." He states, "It is impossible to specify what it is, what it does, or why it has evolved." It seems to be an elusive phenomenon that continues to be explored and studied, and as of yet, it is inconclusive as to how it came to be and how it is always present.

Does Consciousness Have a Source?

Materialism may view consciousness arising from complex interactions of neurons in the brain. Quantum processes occurring in the brain, such as quantum superposition and entanglement, could be what generate subjective experiences. These are hypotheses that have yet to be conclusively proven. These descriptions are expressions emerging from consciousness that cannot be adequately expressed, just as the eye cannot see itself. In my meditation, consciousness (a silent presence of being) is the unexplainable and primordial source.

What is self-consciousness?

Self-consciousness is an ego state of identity that the mind alters and assigns an observing element of awareness to imagine itself in the mind, like the images reflected in a mirror. It's a manifestation of consciousness transformed into an independent agent (ego) that becomes aware of itself as an observer, conceptually and physically. Physically, it conjoins this mental state to assume its residence within the body, possibly the brain or the heart.

The observing Self sees the body and the mind as a vehicle. The body is like a machine that provides a sensory experience through its faculties of perception. The mind is the cognitive experience that manifests appearances of mental phenomena. The observing factor of the mind and the body is an integrated field of energies and vibrations in consciousness that perceives a fabricated reality of mental conceptualizations.

Mentally, the egoic mind is a conceptual and imaginary aspect that manifests from the content of the subconscious mind. Egoic thought content constructs meaningful concepts of itself that create the idea of its existence in the mind, and it attempts to experience a persona that can see and experience itself. The self as the mind (ego) is fabricated and fictitious, although it seems to have an experience of itself as being real. This type of self-consciousness is ego-consciousness, not the Absolute Self or Pure Consciousness beyond the mind and ego.

What is Awareness?

Awareness is like a mirror reflecting images of what the body and mind experience as subjective and objective appearances of reality. Two aspects of awareness exist simultaneously: "relative awareness" and "absolute awareness."

Relative awareness is a field in which phenomenal appearances and disappearances of objects, both physical and mental, come and go in the realm of space and time, cognized by the mind's intellect, imagination, and conceptualization. It manifests fabricated views of conscious experiences where subjects and objects appear and disappear in the present moment.

Another definition of relative awareness is a state of consciousness in which one is an observer, aware of all things that appear and disappear in the mind. It involves knowledge, perception, an understanding of oneself and one's surroundings, and information regarding past experiences and events.

Absolute awareness is empty of any conceptual thoughts, objects, or relative content. The mind cannot understand it because it exists outside of the mind. In many circles, it is thought of as being synonymous with consciousness.

Whereas relative awareness is an energetic field that illuminates all appearances and disappearances of everything, absolute awareness is like an empty mental field where appearances and disappearances are absent. What appears in awareness as objects are relative and doesn't affect consciousness in any way. Awareness is like a mirror that reflects images but doesn't become the images it reflects. The mirror is neutral to any reflective appearances.

In other words, awareness is an undefined and unexplained state of being. I call this state of being a "silent presence," which is an absolute knowing beyond what the mind can understand. It's experienced intuitively. This silent presence of awareness is not an object nor a subject. It is neither, so it is beyond any conceptual thought that attempts to understand it through language or conceptual thinking.

Conclusively, awareness is the illuminating aspect of relative and absolute consciousness in an empty energy field similar to a blank screen or space. The nature of awareness is that it is not an object that the mind can observe. It illuminates everything, including the mind and body, and enables everything to be projected onto its screen. It is not affected by any conditions or events, as it doesn't take on the form of that which it is aware of. In this sense, awareness enables the projection of subjective or objective appearances to come into view in a mental field where subjects and objects come and go. These projections do not affect awareness during their appearances.

Self Awareness

Self-awareness is a conceptualization in which the ego is aware of itself as an imagined person. It is experienced cognitively as a self-reflecting mirror of mental and physical subjects and objects. Attachment to what appears in self-awareness may be mistaken for the authentic view of the Absolute Self.

When awareness is objectified as the agent of association and identification, all perceptions, including memory, reflect personal traits and conceptual information as a mental appearance of the person you "think" you are. When your awareness is turned inward, as in meditation, you become self-aware of your ego identity and begin to see it as a mental fabrication within an imagined reality.

Therefore, self-awareness reflects a conceptualized person's awareness of himself as an object. It is a field of self-consciousness that is a cognitive field reflecting abstract and phenomenal experiences that the mind observes as one's fabricated self.

What is the Source of Awareness?

I don't see that awareness has a source. I think of it as a source of manifestation, just as consciousness is the source. Awareness and consciousness are one connective fabric of existence that emerges from an incomprehensible entity. Consciousness is the source of all existence, and awareness is the field of consciousness where the manifestation of subjects/objects is illuminated into existence. An empty mind is the same as an empty awareness that observes what comes and goes. It is essentially all the same thing, and as a source, it cannot be described or defined. Consciousness is like the ocean; awareness is like the ocean's surface, and appearances are like ripples or waves on the surface. All are ocean! All are consciousness!

Objects come into existence when the light of awareness is focused on them. They're created by the energy that has taken the form of mental or physical appearances. When awareness becomes rarified, it creates an object to be aware of. Thus, it has a creative aspect that can also be elusive and susceptible to imaginative thought.

Pure Naked Awareness

Pure awareness is not clothed in any conceptual idea. It has no inherent qualities that can be described or defined. It is Absolute and is not changeful. It is neither dynamic nor static and is beyond dualist thinking. The same awareness that you were born with is the same awareness that will continue at the death of the body.

Awareness doesn't have a body or a mind; therefore, it is not a creation of something that exists phenomenally. The paradox is that awareness may exist conceptually in one's mind but not when the mind is in a nonconceptual state. It is beyond this dualism. Pure naked awareness is like infinite space. It doesn't have a position or place where it exists. It is not here or there. It also lacks any dualistic characteristics or dynamics of existence or nonexistence, as these are the extremes of conceptual thought. It doesn't know anything like this or that. It is a pure field of emptiness in which subjects and objects appear and disappear as in a mirror. Awareness is an illuminating characteristic of consciousness.

Awareness is empty of conceptual thought when the mind is empty, rendering all appearances with no inherent substance. This doesn't mean that everything ceases to exist. Here, the "I am" declaration of existence may come into play. The concept "I am" is without a predicate, alleviating any idea of an object; thus, it transcends any duality. The inherent awareness, undefined, is the awareness that doesn't have a conceptually conceived notion about itself. It is the Absolute in a formless state with no conceptual knowledge relative to anything. It is just an empty field where all possibilities may emerge.

Abiding in Pure Awareness

To abide in pure awareness is to settle into the illuminating aspect of consciousness when it is not reflecting any images mentally or physically. Awareness is empty of any subjects or objects. In this, a pure clarity of illumination is the light of consciousness. It's an inherent aspect of consciousness that is the substratum of all that appears and disappears.

To abide in this pure awareness is identifying and "being" the awareness as one's residence. Here, even though appearances come and go, one is this substratum, not identifying with any manifestation that appears in its light. It is irrelevant whether something appears or not. This is abiding in pure naked awareness as appearances come and go.

Pathways of Spiritual Awareness

There are many pathways to become awakened and free of the unconscious clutches of the matrices of verbal language. How to do this is controversial in many cultures, religions, and spiritual paths. It requires much intention and attention to become aware of one's desires, attachments, and beliefs. It requires self-inquiry, exploration of one's true self, and testing what is revealed in reality. This self-inquiry of seeing is what the Buddhists call one's "sadhana," or spiritual practice. This is a journey of becoming aware of every aspect of your mind and what you are attached to. Here, one observes one's thoughts, emotions, and behavior while abiding in empty awareness.

First, you take a position of being an observer of all that appears and disappears in awareness. To see clearly, one must abide in awareness and be empty of conceptual thinking. Only then can one see and know what's real and not real. Secondly, you ask your mind, "Who is witnessing or observing the one who is observing all of this?" This question is unanswerable when language is suspended and the mind is empty of conceptual thought. By repeatedly looking into your mind to answer this question without words, you have to look but don't touch and don't fabricate anything conceptually. In other words, whatever appears in your mind is left alone and not grasped. When you look into your mind and see what's there without any thoughts or concepts, you discover that your awareness cannot be an object of itself;

it's presence is recognized when there are no conditions of the mind fabricating an experience.

Insightful experiences of pure awareness and consciousness emerge when one inquires who is aware of the observer. This inquiry has no conceptual answer because the inquirer is not definable and is not a person or a concept. It has to be seen by the inner eye of awareness, which is the awareness itself.

Also, the teachings of Ramana Maharshi, an Indian Guru, involve asking oneself, " Who am I?" This is a mental inquiry used as a mantra that is repeatedly asked by the mind as a meditation practice. Without answering the question with words or thoughts, you see what's there without conceptual thinking. When the question, "Who am I?" is repeated, the mind becomes one-pointed and silences all thoughts, and what is revealed is the silent presence of one's true self, unconditioned.

Also, using the term "I am" as a mantra, repeating it over and over in meditation, is an inquiry with no definition or answer. The term "I am" has no predicate, so it can't be defined or known as an object. "I am" confirms one's identity as the Absolute Self, revealed in silence.

As mentioned, your desires, preferences, and beliefs provide a roadmap of what has been conditioned consciously and unconsciously to produce your conceptual mind. To gain visibility, you must be able to "see" or transcend what has been hidden from view and conditioned as the conceptual mind. Observing your behavior and meditation are the most effective ways to bring this conditioning into conscious awareness. Initially, it involves experiencing oneself as the observer being aware of observing. This mindfulness method can be applied to sustaining an even posture amid activity. It's a mindfulness meditation in action. Many more paths provide a practice that will increase one's awareness and relieve the mind of conceptualization.

Chapter 17: Mindfulness and Spiritual Awareness

Chapter 17

Mindfulness and Spiritual Awareness

Mindfulness and spiritual awareness are closely intertwined concepts, each enhancing and deepening the other on their journey towards a fuller understanding of oneself and the world around them. While distinct, they share a common ground of nonjudgmental observation and acceptance of the present moment.

Mindfulness

Mindfulness directs our attention to the current moment, paying close attention to our thoughts, feelings, bodily sensations, and surroundings without judgment. It involves letting go of past anxieties and future worries, anchoring ourselves in the here and now. It also concentrates on whatever actions are being performed in the present moment. It may also be called the "Zen

Mind," meaning that the wholeness of experiencing the present moment is aligned with the actions that one is engaged in exclusively, without distraction. When the mind is full of emptiness it can be focused exclusively on the task at hand and not be distracted by discursive thought. Mindfulness means it is full of emptiness.

Instead of resisting our experiences, mindfulness encourages open and accepting observation. We acknowledge our thoughts and emotions without attachment, allowing them to flow without getting caught up in their narrative. Through sustained practice, mindfulness cultivates a heightened awareness of our internal and external landscape. We begin to see patterns in our thoughts and behaviors, understand our triggers, and gain insights into our true selves.

Living in Mindfulness

Mindfulness living entails being attentive to what appears in the present moment "as it is" without engaging in it conceptually. To live in mindfulness as an empty mind, you cannot say that you know anything as being this or that, conceptually. When you see physical and mental appearances "as they are," you see and respond spontaneously and intuitively with the appropriate and "right action."

As one's awareness expands, all becomes revealed about what is inaccurate or being misrepresented. In the present moment, everything appears as it is and is not what the thinking mind imagines. This truth is beyond thinking of what's true and untrue, as these are only concepts. When the truth is seen silently, without conceptual thought, it is recognized as the "silent presence" of what is appearing in the present moment. Once known, you can rejoice in what you have always been - the "Absolute" reality beyond conceptual or dualistic thinking. "Silent presence" is apparently who we are.

Spiritual Awareness

Spiritual awareness goes beyond individual experience, seeking a connection to something greater than oneself. This could be a divine being, a universal consciousness, or a deep sense of interconnectedness with nature and all living things. A central aspect of spiritual awareness is life's search for meaning and purpose. It involves contemplating our place in the universe, asking questions about existence, and aligning our actions with our core values.

As we connect with something more significant, a sense of compassion naturally arises. We become more sensitive to the suffering of others and develop a desire to act with kindness and understanding.

Spiritual awareness is beyond conceptual thinking or past and future concepts. When the small self is relinquished for the big Self, all is one, and one is all. Beyond conceptual imagination and fabrication lies a world devoid of separation, division, selfishness, and self-identities. An egoless mind is an empty mind. There's no one there to experience it. It is the experience itself, and each event leaves no trace. You are the present moment in its totality. Spontaneously, "being" the unknown and the undefined presence of the present moment is our natural self just being its Self.

Mindfulness Supports Spiritual Awakening

Mindfulness helps quiet our minds' constant chatter, creating space for a deeper connection with ourselves and the divine. It allows us to tap into a sense of stillness and peace that fosters spiritual awakening.

By observing our thoughts and emotions without judgment, we see the illusion of the ego and naturally connect with our authentic selves - the Absolute Self. This deeper understanding opens us to experiencing the Divine within.

Mindfulness cultivates a state of receptivity and awakening, making us more open to spiritual experiences and insights. Through this openness, we become more aware of synchronicities, guidance, and insights from beyond the egoic realm.

Ultimately, mindfulness and spiritual awareness are not exclusive paths but complementary forces working together on our journey of self-discovery. Mindfulness provides the tools for present-moment awareness and inner exploration, while spiritual awareness guides us toward connection, meaning, and a deeper understanding of our place in the universe.

Chapter 18

Spiritual Practices and Rituals

Meditation

To relieve the mind of conceptual thought, one can practice meditation. Meditation eliminates all identifications and attachments to external and internal objects in one's mental awareness. It transcends conceptual thinking by experiencing a silent space that is not internal or external. Silent meditation eliminates conceptual thinking; the mind abides in empty awareness and is not concerned with external or internal phenomena. It becomes empty, still, and silent. A dispassionate and quiet mind reveals a natural presence of being that is not fabricated in any way. It is relieved of the dualistic nature of language and is transcendent to any intellectual concepts.

Meditation doesn't try to silence the mind; this happens effortlessly over time. The mind's function is to 'think thoughts' to define, describe, and attempt to understand what is appearing and disappearing. This thinking apparatus is what we are accustomed to all the time. So, initially, it will probably feel unnatural to experience a silent mind, and you may feel like this is an impossible or tedious task.

If you persist in this meditation effort, you begin to relax into a state of pure awareness, where thought creation subsides by itself. Contemplation and meditation are prerequisites to knowing what the mind is and what is unknowable conceptually.

When the mind is empty, pure awareness is felt to be the "ground of one's existence." When one is absorbed into this ground of being, one is said to be in a state of samadhi, i.e., pure, undifferentiated, and unconditioned awareness. This is a pure state of expanded consciousness that permeates awareness without the distractions of the mind. This pure state is not an event or an experience since it has yet to be fabricated or imagined. It is the ground of being that is always naturally present.

When there is no mental activity from the past, present, or future, the observant "I" becomes the now-moment, silently and unconditioned. It is an effortless presence that becomes evident to be one's natural Self and is egoless, without identity or attachment. It is an effortless awareness that sees itself appear and disappear as multiple subjects and objects.

Meditation is not an experience, event, or something that can be attained. Meditation is letting go of all ambitions and efforts to attempt to achieve something, and it is settling into one's awareness without grasping any thoughts, concepts, etc. The authentic self is beyond the body and mind or any matrix of conceptual thinking. Beliefs, imaginations, and ideas cannot define the authentic self. Thus, the authentic self cannot be comprehended by the conceptual mind. At least, this is my experience. Meditation goes beyond conceptual thinking, where the mind is experienced as a presence of silence.

Discursive thought, or logical or analytical thinking, is a fundamental way of processing information and understanding the world around us. When discursive thinking subsides, the mind abides in its natural nonconceptual state of oneness and awareness. To realize or know this, one has to go beyond mental or intellectual comprehension. This entails entering an unknown state of being, imperceivable to the body or the conceptual mind. An imaginary mind or a mind that fabricates experiences doesn't abide in the Absolute Self. One must know that the conceptual mind exists as thoughts, fabrications of a symbolic representation of 'what is,' which inherently has no intrinsic value or substance. The mind cannot comprehend absolute awareness, just as the eye cannot see itself. So, seeing one's authentic self cannot be an object of knowledge. This is why the ego cannot experience self-realization.

Returning to my disclaimer: I referenced Einstein's statement that realization or awakening cannot be achieved when attempting to have the experience from the very mind that can't comprehend it. That is to know that this is a state of "being" that is always silently present and hidden from the conceptual mind. This presence is free of any conceptual activity in the mind, and the universal manifestation of 'what is' appears and disappears in our awareness, and it doesn't come with a definition or verbal commentary.

The presence of consciousness is the center of everything that exists and does not exist simultaneously. The cohesive substance of pure consciousness unifies everything as the oneness, the wholeness, and the true unfabricated nature of all things. You might equate it to the quantum field, where infinite possibilities in all of their versions are present and where the manifestation of everything in creation exists and doesn't exist simultaneously. You are That!

There are many forms of meditation and many spiritual paths that advocate meditation as a practice for enlightenment. There's silent meditation, mindfulness meditation, Vipassana meditation, Bhakti or devotional meditation, and hundreds or thousands more. Meditation can also be prayer.

Most meditations have the same intention regarding an outcome. They are practiced to silence the mind from conceptual thinking and unite us with an authentic experience of our true selves. No subject meditates on an object, as the subject and object are the same when thoughts subside. Continued practice enables the mind to become focused, concentrated, and one-pointed, allowing the meditator to concentrate on letting go of thoughts and distractions.

Devotional Meditation is for those devoted to an enlightened person, a God, a higher being, or some spiritual entity worshipped in some devotional way. In my practice, I initially thought I was a devotional meditator and that my practice was to be devoted to my Guru or a Divine Being such as God. As I practiced this way, I began to see that I was conceptually fabricating an experience of devotion. I was continuously immersed in conceptual thought related to the source or subject. This didn't stand true for me, and my feelings did not align with my intentions or practice. My intuition led me to see that this meditation was not my "cup of tea."

Bhakti Yoga is the continuous contemplation of the Absolute Self or Brahman (interpreted as God). It is not a conceptual practice or an experience. The reflection of the pure, Absolute Self is a mindful state of mind that is adhered to continuously. It is knowing and being one's true Self as the only thing that exists. This knowing comes from the experience of being that is effortless and is not experienced as an event or action. The continuous contemplation of one's Self denies any sense of fabrications or imaginations of existing as an identity. It is just a knowing and being the Absolute without a conceptual mind comprehending it. This meditation is experiencing the Absolute presence as a silent 'be-ness.'

Mindfulness Meditation is a wonderful practice for abiding in and experiencing the present moment. This practice of being in the present moment 'as it is' is the best way to have a consistent transactional experience of reality. This meditation transcends any concepts of past and future. This is a meditative experience that everyone should practice regardless of their path.

Mindfulness means to have focused and dedicated attention placed on the present moment without verbal judgments or conceptual analysis. Accepting all that appears and disappears in the present moment is experienced as one's life, just 'as it is.' I prefer to call this meditation "mindless" since the mind is empty of conceptual thought, and its mindfulness is full of emptiness. It's Okay to be mindless or to lose your mind if you can find one!

Silent Meditation is my current practice. Over the 60 years of meditation, I found that any fabricated experience of meditation does not reveal an absolute truth that is sustainable. Most meditators will find this meditation the most difficult because the mind doesn't want to be silent. It's not in its nature. To still the mind is like training a wild horse. It doesn't want to be trained. It took a long time to condition my mind to be dispassionate about attachments and preferences, some of which still pops up frequently.

Silent meditation begins with the surrender of a thinking person, contrary to how we were brought up and educated. Whenever a thought appears, we should ask, "Who is thinking this thought?" Each time you ask the question, stop, look, and listen without conceptually fabricating anything in the mind. Can you find a thinker? Without a thinker, who is present that experiences a conceptualized reality?

We can refine our thinking process to navigate our lives in harmony with whatever appears in our reality. If you consistently practice silent meditation, you can sustain a harmonious relationship with subjective and objective realities. This is only possible when you are genuinely free of any desire to be or not to be a person. It is paradoxical.

To accomplish silent meditation requires several aspects to be developed (at least in my case):

- I had to alleviate any fearful ideas that I would lose my body and mind, existentially.
- I had to be dedicated, committed, and have complete faith that this was possible for

my well-being and make it okay to lose my identity.

- I had to surrender all concepts of ego-identification, even the idea that a person is meditating or is on a spiritual path.

In doing so, it is a letting go experience that alleviates all identities of myself and reveals an unknown and undefined existence. I had to get comfortable not knowing anything, which is contrary to any intelligent person's reasoning. By doing this for many years, my mind began to get quiet. I began to see a silent presence of being and existence that is not dependent upon any thoughts or identification. It is an experience where there is no person there to experience anything. It is the present moment expressed in one's mind without a fabricated person.

So, what I am describing here is what I've referred to as a conceptual realization. The mind realizes it is on a path that cannot attain its goal, i.e., enlightenment. When this conceptual realization occurs, the mind relaxes its hold on one's mental and transactional experiences. It becomes subservient to being a silent presence in a natural state of pure awareness. Thus, the wild horse is tamed! It stops seeking and grasping for anything.

There's a saying in Buddhist scriptures that if one meets the Buddha on the path, one must slay him. This means that the attachment to one's practice must also be surrendered. The attachment to a path or the teacher becomes ritualistic, and one's practice becomes a delusion with conceptual conditions. This is an obstacle to enlightenment and must also be relinquished.

I can be silently aware and still participate in this transactional experience of worldly life. I can be in the world but not identified with it. I began seeing that most of my attachments and desires were irrelevant to what was real or not or what was required for my participation. Thus, a detached view is experienced just as an actor plays a role in a movie. The actor knows it is not real but plays the role as if it is.

A Guided Meditation to Silence the Mind

Sit comfortably with the spine erect and aligned with your body vertically. An erect posture is conducive to staying awake and not falling asleep. You can sit in a chair or in a yoga meditation posture.

Pay attention to your breathing. Don't take big breaths. With your mind, observe the inhalation and exhalation of your breath. Don't try to control the rate of your breathing. If it's fast or slow, let it be whatever it is. Let your breathing go by itself. The body will take care of it and will take oxygen when needed. Don't inhale until the body needs to. Just let go at the end of the exhalation and let there be a pause. The body will initiate the inhalation when it needs oxygen, and then it will begin by itself. You don't have to try to breathe. Let the body do the breathing. Let your breath go, and your breathing will become very shallow, and that's okay.

One breathing cycle is an inhalation and an exhalation:

- Let the body take in air by itself. This will happen automatically.

- After the inhalation, don't hold onto the air. Let the exhalation go immediately when you have taken in the air the body needs. It's automatic.

- Don't immediately take another breath at the end of the exhalation. Pause (if you can) and let the exhalation pause; wait until the body needs oxygen, and let the inhalation begin by itself.

- Repeat this without distraction. You'll begin to see that the space between breaths at the end of every exhalation gets longer and longer.

- Stay in this silent space between breaths and between thoughts. This is a space of silence, empty of conceptual thinking. Let thoughts come and go, but don't engage in them. Let them pass like clouds in the sky and ignore them. They are irrelevant. Marinate your mind in this silent space between breaths and thoughts and let go of everything, even your existence.

Another Meditative Focus:

Focus on your heart chakra or heart center in the middle of your chest or the third eye chakra, the space just above and between your eyes, in the center of your forehead. Begin breathing in one of these centers. Feel the sensation of breathing in the third eye or heart chakras. Stay focused on this and only pay attention to breathing in this center. The breathing will begin to slow down. Don't try to control it. Your mantra during this meditation should be "Let go," "Let go," and "Let go" every time you exhale. Your breathing may become so shallow that you may not feel as though you are breathing at all. This is normal.

Another Meditative Focus:

Focus your mind on who is breathing. Observe your breathing and look inside your mind to see who is observing it. Is there a person watching your breathing? Or is breathing just happening by itself? Without thinking about being the observer, silently look and see who or what is observing your breathing. What is the presence that observes your breathing? Silently, let your breath go by itself. Is there a silent presence of just being? Is this the awareness of a 'presence' that is silent? Who is being silent? Just look and don't try to answer these questions with your mind or words. See what's there when the mind is not thinking. Don't try to stop thoughts from arising; just ignore them.

Another Meditative Focus:

Pay close attention to this presence. It's a silent presence that is not thinking. If a thought arises, ask who the thinker of this thought is, and then be quiet and look to see who's thinking. Don't use any words or language to answer any of these questions. Just look silently, not focused on any one thing. Can you find a thinker?

When you're silent, there is no thinker—a quiet presence of being remains, not a fabrication or concept. Stay focused on this presence and let it be by itself. Let it absorb your mind and body. Surrender everything to this presence and abide in it as your true self.

Stay silently present, alert, and awake. There's nothing to do and nothing to see or experience here. The mind is empty, and awareness is pure without any appearances. Let everything be as it is without commentary. Once absorbed in this presence of the unknown, you will be in a state of samadhi or nirvana, as it is called. It is effortless!

Many practices and different paths will assist in merging the mind into an expanded awareness without conceptual thinking and allowing one to experience one's true Self.

Practice of Service and Karma Yoga

The practice of service is to serve the universe for the benefit and well-being of everyone and everything. When you see that you are not separate from everything else, you realize that your existence is connected to everything in the universe. This connection is realized when the mind is silenced, and the silent presence of being diminishes the personal ego. It's not an idea. Your body and mind are all the bodies and minds that appear simultaneously. When you know this, you will be of service to yourself and everyone else.

This practice develops the awareness of compassion that enables one to see a perspective according to how others see themselves and how you can serve their well-being. To be in service requires a practice of intentional adherence to creating an environment of well-being for all creatures and objects that appear in the now-moments of your life.

Imagine you are serving everyone as if you were serving yourself. And no reciprocity is required. You wouldn't be expected to be rewarded or praised for your actions. This practice adheres to this commitment to serve the universe in the best way possible without any attachment to the results of your actions. This is what is called true Karma Yoga in practice.

This is how I see it. It's just about staying in the flow without expectations and attachments. It's also about givers and takers, but that's another topic of discussion that I'll skip for now.

The Practice of Gratitude

Gratitude is a positive action that may result from the awareness attained through meditation and service. It is a compassionate, loving, and grateful way of seeing what appears and disappears in one's life. It is a very high state of awareness that consists of the highest values, as seen through the eyes of adoration and wonder for all creation.

When there is only gratitude, any possibility of negativity or agitation will automatically disappear from your mind. Negative behavior and negative emotions cannot co-exist when gratitude is present.

To be thankful for all of existence is to live a life of love, joy, and compassion. Gratitude is a cohesive and comprehensive experience that unifies one's existence with the universe. It attracts energies that are universally responsive to creating positive outcomes.

Happiness

Consciousness is happiness and is happy all the time! The ego can lose this inherent happiness because of its conditions and preferences, such as frustration, a lack of something desired, discontentment, stress and anxiety, etc. Happiness is effortless when there are no conditions or preferences. Nothing has to be added or taken away to be happy. If you are always trying to add or remove something, thinking it will make you happy or happier, you will be mistaken, and this will be an obstacle to your realization and understanding of who you are.

Religious Practices

Religion is an extraordinary field of spiritual practice that has expanded around the globe. Many such religions advocate some form of moral and ethical ideologies and practices. I see that most churches inspire and instill good ethics and morals in their congregants. I realized that almost every religion and their religious or spiritual scriptures expound the same thing: good vs evil, peace on earth, being a silent presence, gratitude and service, and much more.

The problem that religions have is when they become political. Some church institutions have engaged in manipulation to control their congregants in many ways. Here, one has to be cautious not to get trapped by the conditional aspects of a particular religion. Most religions are dogmatic and ritualistic in their beliefs and, therefore, can be a diversion to one's spiritual growth if one becomes attached to its surface appearances and takes all of it literally. Could it be that each religion's scriptures are pretty accurate and primarily seek their members' well-being? The problem is when religions become politicized, they become radicalized. Fanatical and obsessive behavior ensues!

Devotion to an ideology or religious doctrine is beneficial when the devotee becomes aligned with the essence of their teachings. It's more a result of gaining insights and actualizing personal experience of the teachings. And, it is not through intellectualizing a fabrication of misrepresentations.

The religious practice of surrendering to a higher being or dimension is a transcendental insight that expands awareness. This enables the recognition of one's identity to feel the oneness with all of existence. Here, the self is one with the higher presence of being. The ego subsides when the silent self realizes that the idea of the "I" self is false and never existed in the first place. The realized Self exists as the nonverbal expression of the present moment and is not a conceptual or relative experience. It is the presence of a silent being that exists by itself. One's true Self sees itself as what it knows to be. It is one! It is God! And you are That, without a doubt!

Religious Rituals

Religious rituals can focus and align our religious practice by consistently directing our attention to sustain our spiritual exploration and avoid distraction. For instance, using rosary beads is a ritualistic practice where a prayer or mantra is repeated with each rosary bead. This keeps the mind focused on an object and develops concentration and attentiveness that help us stay in the present moment.

Rituals can be designed to trigger specific mental states by programming a conditional response into the subconscious, where the experience becomes automatic and habitual when a particular prompt is articulated. For instance, I feel a presence of silence and peace that never changes. If I create a guided meditation to practice this every day, I can use the entire guidance by consolidating and associating it with one word. This word will automatically trigger the meditative experience provided and associate it with the actual state of being the "silent presence" abiding in the true Self. The experience will follow if it's been programmed into the subconscious mind.

This is how a mantra concentrates the mind on one word or phrase that provides a universal vibration and meaning that unifies and integrates all existence into one thing, perceptually and existentially. Aum is one such mantra that is a primordial sound and expression of the Absolute.

Understanding and realizing that the spiritual path is not the rituals themselves is crucial. They are only tools. You may use a boat to get from one side of a river to the other. The boat will bring you to the other side, but you don't have to take it with you once there. It's discarded, and its function has been used for its intended purpose. It's the same with meditation.

Meditation is a concept. Meditation is the empirical realization of who you are. Once that is accomplished, you'll not have to practice meditation regularly, and it will become more optional. You're no longer engaged in a search or trying to discover something. Why would one continue to search for something it already discovered and that was always there all the time? Not that you would discontinue meditation entirely. In fact, your meditation becomes your life's experiences in the present moment. All is one and one is all! This is a continuous realization that actualizes one's experiences as "the presence of being."

If you are participating and engaging in your subjective and objective reality, it may be necessary to sit in meditation when your mind has become distracted or disassociated with your true nature. You may feel that you've become entangled in irrelevant circumstances or distractions you don't want to be engaged in. Or, you don't want to be thinking or acting in some drama. This may be an excellent time to sit and be silent and still. Here, you are not thinking, not seeking, not knowing, and just being. The mind returns to a state of clarity when it has been flushed. If your day begins with meditation, it will regulate all bodily functions and provide clarity of mind that will benefit your daily activities. Your mind will be more focused and alert to function at a higher level of awareness and concentration.

It's not a question of whether you attained anything or not or whether you discovered anything. You begin to see that nothing needs to be added or subtracted that will reveal or enhance this presence of "be-ness."

There's only one thing to say, "I simply don't know! I can't know! And I'm comfortable not knowing!" The egoic "I" person cannot know itself as a person or anything else.

Chapter 19: Enlightenment – Nirvana – Awakening

Chapter 19

What is Enlightenment and Self-Realization?

Self-Realization

Self-Realization is not a state of consciousness. The true and Absolute Self is synonymous with pure consciousness, the fabric of existence and nonexistence. Consciousness is self-knowing itself, which means it is independent of any conceptual or physical experience. The conceptual egoic person believes it is separate from everything else. It doesn't exist, and any knowledge of this is purely conceptual or fabricated; there cannot be something known as a person other than a conceptual idea of one.

Only the Self can know itself. When the Self realizes who it is, it sees its true nature and can no longer be identified as separate from anything. Any separate identity is dissolved. When you become fully aware of your Absolute identity, you see the present moment as your Self, always devoid of conceptual thinking. Your true identity is the unconditioned present moment. The "presence" of the true Self cannot be created or destroyed because it never came into existence. It has always been silently present and was hidden by the veil of the egoic mind.

Knowing your authentic Self is when there is nothing to be known. You cannot know your true Self as a concept or a thought. It is not a subject or object. There's nothing to know, and knowing nothing is impossible! How can you know nothing because nothing doesn't exist? If nothing is non-existent, then you cannot exist either. As mentioned, nothing means "no thing".

When you let go of any identification with the mind, ego, and body, an effortless transcendence of self-identity emerges. No thoughts of "I," "me," "mine", etc. All fabricated realities are seen to be false imaginations. They are conceptual ideas and beliefs; when this insight is experienced, realization occurs, and you are fully awakened to your true Self. When the true Self becomes tired of playing a role in life that is not true, it begins to realize it is not the identity that the thinking mind has associated it with. The true and Absolute Self is beyond something that exists or doesn't exist.

Some may think that silencing the mind is the goal. As mentioned, nothing can be done by the mind. The Self has to realize itself non-dualistically and without intellectual knowledge or understanding. In other words, without the idea of you and the ideas you are attached to or about who you think you are.

It is said that Self-realization only happens through grace. That was my experience, and I found it to be true. The enlightened awakening, combined with the frustrations of every effort to attain the unattainable, happens when an authentic surrendering and letting go occurs, completing the cycles of what is known and not known. Looking back, you'll see that grace was eminently present throughout your journey.

After seeing with a non-conceptual mind, you'll no longer be able to affirm or negate anything. You can honestly say, "I don't know anything and don't have to know anything." If the present-moment reality is necessary for something to be known for one's participation in this phenomenon, it will provide the required thoughts or physical resources to appear synchronistically. Your conceptual toolbox of thought creation can be used when engaging oneself in transactional experiences within this phenomenal existence. Enlightenment doesn't negate anything or affirm anything. Your participation and engagement in this phenomenon take on an entirely different role when the absence of a conceptual identity is realized, providing one's existence as not a fabricated idea of a body or a mind.

The Path to Self-Realization

The path of self-realization can be very disturbing, frustrating, and even fearful for some of us. The ego is the main obstacle. It does not want to give up its autonomy and its controlling power. Creating and developing who you think and believe you are took many years. So now, why would you want to disassociate yourself from it? Many will not go down this path of inquiry and discovery for fear of losing their self-identity and thinking they may even lose their mind.

If the fabricated ego ("I") believes it is on a path to self-realization, it will pursue self-realization as a task or problem that has to be solved. And the conceptual mind will immediately begin the pursuit. After much effort, the conceptual or ego mind eventually surrenders when it can't experience self-realization, as every effort has been exhausted. The ego can't experience self-realization because it is the true Self that realizes the ego is fictitious, a conceptual identity, and it doesn't exist. That's what the realization is!

In the final realization, the true Self realizes and knows itself to be consciousness, empty of any thought content. In other words, language cannot define oneself as existing or not. These are just extreme concepts. Only pure consciousness knows that all appearances and disappearances are unsubstantial when defined by conceptual thought.

When the ego is not present, there is a silent presence of being that is not construed by the mind. Thus, an empty mind removes the thoughts of a person's existence and the mind itself. No thoughts - no ego - no mind! In this sense, it is a death and resurrection. The veil of ignorance is torn away, and what's left is unexplainable. It is felt as a presence of a silent being. Here, one loses one's fabricated mind, and the mind becomes empty of any existential experience of itself. It is beyond existence and nonexistence and is always present. Nothing is here, there, or anywhere.

Can Self-Realization be Explained or Described?

Self-realization, ignorance, and illusion doesn't exist. They are purely conceptual fabrications. It is said that the pure Self is beyond Nirvana (enlightenment) and Samsara (Illusion). Their existence or nonexistence are just concepts;

even self-realization doesn't exist, as it is also a concept.

When the mind is at a neutral point of zero, it lacks subjects and objects. What's present in the now-moment is not defined or labeled and is seen as "not this" or "not that" when thoughts arise in the mind. This is our undifferentiated consciousness that is always present. The human senses or the conceptual mind can never perceive it. It is not discovered or recognized because what's revealed is a formless Self, which the mind can't see. The Self realizes itself; no person is realizing the Self. Essentially, the Self returns to Itself as its inseparable identity. A wave in the ocean appears and then subsides back into the sea and is never separated from it. The separated ego-identity never existed, and what appeared to exist subsides back into the formless Self.

This presence exists by itself without adding or subtracting anything. It exists independently of the mind and body. The mind and body are phenomenal manifestations within the Self as an imagined existence, like a dream. It can be experienced as an optical illusion, where physical and mental appearances manifest like mirages in a desert. Nothing can be explained or defined conceptually as truth in this phenomenon.

Realization happens by itself and is like a flower blooming. If one tries to open a flower bud, it will be damaged or die. The same is true of the mind attempting to attain it. This can be disturbing, frustrating, and even fearful for the ego.

How to Realize the Self

How to realize the Self is paradoxical. You cannot attain it regardless of how much effort you put into seeking it. Trying to achieve it will always be futile. Its attainment is said to happen by the efforts made in one's spiritual practices, like meditation. This is true! And it is also not true! This paradox is understood by the attempt to attain it and the effortless state of pure being that reveals it. Most of us have to go through the process of trying and searching until we become intellectually exhausted and frustrated. Before we finally surrender the ego, we become dispassionate about it. At this point, it comes down to two options: suicide or pursuing self-realization.

Letting go of all that the mind has fabricated allows the ego to be absorbed by the Absolute pure consciousness. And this surrender provides a life of peace and happiness. An attitude or posture of living this life as if we are dead is a practice that some take on as their spiritual practice.

This sustains a presence of living that is always submissive to know what is not true.

To realize the Self is actually beyond both concepts of effort and effortlessness. The mind is useless as a tool for realization. If you take what the mind says as truth, you'll be dragged into one rabbit hole after another. If I say something like, "I know from personal experience," this statement would be me going down another rabbit hole. The ego can't win!

Even though attachment to the conceptual mind is the problem, and the problem cannot be solved by the same mindset that created it, conscious awareness of a nonverbal reality emerges and exposes the conceptual ego as a falsehood. All is seen as a fabricated reality that is made up in the mind.

If self-inquiry is applied through persistent observation and contemplation, a conceptual understanding or recognition of one's ego becomes apparent. This understanding will eventually eliminate all egotistical attachments through a gained awareness that eliminates any entanglements of the mind to think it is a real person. Self-inquiry in this context is to turn the mind inward, not letting it go out through the senses to experience anything external. Holding the mind inward enables one to see what appears in the mind and what thoughts are causing action or inaction. One can sense the silent presence that permeates all existence when the mind is empty of thoughts.

Even though the mind is useless in this effort, most aspirants must practice meditation or some other method to attain it. This is the paradox. You must exhaust every possibility to attain it, and then it will reveal itself.

As the ego surrenders to the incomprehensible Absolute, its dominance over the mind subsides, revealing all that is untrue; the Self then realizes itself to be what it has always been and has always prevailed as the primordial source of everything. It was always present and was never created.

Self-realization is only possible if Grace unlocks the secrets and insights of what's real and what's not. Grace is showered upon the aspirant when humility and vulnerability are predominant. This opens the door to surrendering.

Chapter 20

Grace and Synchronicity

What is Grace?

In religious contexts, the literal meaning of grace often evolves to denote undeserved favor or support, usually from a higher power. This understanding has its roots in Latin, where "gratia" meant "favor" or "thanks." This meaning is particularly prevalent in Christianity, where grace is seen as God's unmerited love and forgiveness bestowed upon humans. Grace, at its core, signifies receiving something beautiful and beneficial without having earned or strived for it. It's a windfall, a stroke of luck, a serendipitous encounter that enriches our lives unexpectedly. This understanding resonates across various cultures and belief systems.

Grace often signifies God's love and blessings bestowed upon us freely, regardless of our merits or deeds. We cannot earn or bargain for grace. It's a gift offered out of divine love and generosity from the true Self, God.

Grace in my life has always been there. Every experience that I've had was initiated by Grace, whether I was aware of it or not. Grace provided even the negative and hurtful experiences that caused tears. Grace happens when the aspirant is ready to see the truth. When this happens, the mind is turned inwards to commune with one's Universal God, Guru, or higher self and asks for assistance. It opens the door to surrendering.

There is a universal intelligence that is intuitive and all-knowing, and you might consider it God's intelligence. This intelligence provides the experiences we need to remind us of who we are. Its primordial existence is God-consciousness; it is all-inclusive.

Synchronicity: A Dance of Meaningful Coincidences

Synchronicity, coined by psychologist Carl Jung, refers to meaningful coincidences of events that appear unrelated casually but hold significant personal or symbolic meaning. Think of it as the universe orchestrating seemingly random occurrences that resonate deeply with your inner desires, thoughts, or intentions. Self-realization, conversely, is the journey of uncovering your authentic self, true potential, and purpose in life. It's about shedding conditioning, aligning with spiritual values, and living with integrity.

Synchronicities can serve as gentle confirmations that you're on the right path. A chance encounter with an old mentor right when you're feeling lost or finding a book with the exact information you need can nudge you forward with renewed confidence.

Paying attention to synchronicities prompts reflection on your inner world. As you ponder the meaning behind these coincidences, you may uncover hidden desires, fears, or patterns in your thinking that influence your life. Recognizing synchronicities can strengthen your intuition and trust in the unseen forces shaping your life. It fosters a connection to something larger than yourself, encouraging you to tap into your inner wisdom and make courageous choices.

Synchronicities can act as serendipitous gateways to new opportunities and connections. A chance conversation with a stranger that leads to your dream job or finding a lost item with unexpected sentimental value can open doors you never knew existed. Recognizing the subtle dance of synchronicities in your life cultivates an attitude of gratitude for the universe's guidance and support. It encourages acceptance of positive and challenging experiences, knowing they all contribute to your growth.

Much of my research aimed to clarify and deepen my understanding of what needed to be more accurate in my spiritual search. I studied topics such as quantum theory, Hindu, Tibetan, and Zen scriptures, Christian mysticism, and how scientists and spiritual practitioners understand consciousness.

As I researched these topics, I found that many synchronicities provided information or the exact wording of a conceptual point. It seemed like the experience of "channeling" my higher intuition was at play. In my journey, many experiences happened precisely when I needed them.

To summarize, synchronicity can be a powerful tool for self-realization. It's crucial to avoid obsessing over coincidences or interpreting them as definitive proof of any specific path or spiritual experience. Synchronicity is a lens through which you can interpret your journey, not a map dictating every step. Use it as a source of inspiration, guidance, and confirmation, but continue actively engaging with your inner world and making conscious choices toward self-realization. True self-discovery comes through seeing repeatedly that the mind is empty when it is relaxed and in its natural state of silence, peace, and oneness.

Chapter 21

Waking Up From the Dream

Who or What is Awakening?

Awakening is to awaken from the dream of abiding in a conceptual reality and breaking free of its illusions. Becoming aware and seeing that who you "think" you are is not who you really are. It is only a structured matrix of thoughts that have conditioned you to believe you are something you are not. It is the same with Self-realization.

As awareness expands, an awakening begins. It may be sudden or progress over time. Initially, insights will appear that question what you know or think is real. From this, you may start thinking that there must be something more to one's life other than how you're experiencing it. You begin to see that imagining it to be something it isn't is no longer serving you. The mind starts to become aware and experience what is and isn't authentic or genuine about oneself.

Pure awareness reveals an awakening of the mind, and consciousness seems to understand that illusive fabrication has conditioned it to be something it is not. It has been experiencing what may be like a dream. You realize that what has happened to one's consciousness has become a limited and contracted view of existence that is illusory. One wakes up to what is real and what is not. This awakening begins the process of repairing what has been conditioned. Through pure empty awareness, awakening may be an immediate or gradual realization. This journey doesn't have to be difficult, but it is for many.

To see Absolute reality 'as it is' is only possible when no conceptual thoughts, imaginations, or conditioned thought processes occur in the mind. To be awake, one abides in empty awareness effortlessly with no attachment to anything conceived of as a thought. All senses are functioning normally, but no objects of perception are conceptualized. Empty awareness is the presence of being awakened. This is the human's natural state that is always present, and this underlying awareness has always existed and was never created. It's beyond existence and nonexistence. You don't have to act or do anything to be aware. You always are by default!

Chapter 22

Living in the Present Moment

Living in the Present Moment

The importance of living in the present moment and responding to life is when your awareness is untainted by a conceptual reality with an awakened mind that is not attached to anything or anyone. And is content by accepting the present moment as it appears and disappears. Without the attachment to a human language matrix or a digital one, you are free to respond without a conditioned, programmed mind. Reactionary responses emanate from the subconscious mind, determining much of what appears and disappears in your present moment. Thus, freedom from conditioning allows you to make better choices and decisions because the mind has no preconceived ideas, assumptions, or expectations.

We can never know what the present moment is. The minute we say what it is, to affirm or recognize its appearance, it is already an experience that cannot be seen again in the immediacy of the present moment. We only experience the present moment after it happens and after it's processed by our body and mind, after which it then becomes an experience. An experience is something or some event that occurred in the past. We can never experience the present moment directly in real-time. After the senses perceive an object, it is assimilated by the senses and the brain and then processed into a conceptualized experience of what you "think" happened. By the time the senses assimilate and communicate through the mental processing of the brain, the experience can only be known as a memory.

The conceptualization of experiencing the present moment as thoughts impair our ability to experience it accurately, precisely as it is in real time. We "think" we make it real by conceptualizing it existentially and then labeling and categorizing it into our memory, but it can never be a reality again. It can't be experienced twice! A memory is not the same as the experience of it when it happened. Nothing can be experienced twice due to the changing reality as it evolves. Nothing can remain the same, as everything is in constant motion and changes constantly. I'm appalled whenever I hear somebody say, "Been there, done that!" Every instance of the present moment experience is an entirely new instance that is never the same as a previous one. The experience of the present moment can only happen as a stream of consciousness that appears and disappears on the screen of awareness, where all appearances leave no trace or memory.

To live in the present moment is not to live in your thoughts. In silence and emptiness, you see what appears and disappears "as it is." You can move about in this world by just "being," free of the attachment to thoughts without excluding the thinking mind. We have a thinking mind, which is a human characteristic. Thoughts are energetic expressions of what we experience that may be accurate or inaccurate. The freedom from the attachment to it allows everything to exist "as it is," and the mind functions in an aware, awakened state of "being."

I've learned that I can be in a mindful state sustained by an empty mind as my default state. Suppose I interact with my subjective and objective realities precisely as they appear. In that case, I can pull the skill sets of language, memory, and information needed out of my mental toolbox to engage in any interaction. This conscious choice is natural and appropriate for engaging and participating in conceptual realities with the awareness of the underlying truth of "what is" and "who is doing what."

We all have developed ideas and concepts about our reality. Each person has their view of their reality as they see it. There are as many realities as there are humans, each with its reality.

Living in this world functionally and freely is not exclusively opposed to abiding in pure awareness. Attachment, lack of awareness and understanding, and false conditioning cause illusions and delusions. One can live in this world freely by not attaching to anything or anyone and not identifying oneself as a defined person, regardless of whether we are immersed in a conceptual or verbal reality. Identification is the imagined concept that imprisons the mind with fabricated beliefs, desires, and preferences. This creates a sense of attachment, always grasping for something or fearing losing something.

The Now Moment and "Right Action"

The essence of an awakened being is living in the now-moment with "right action," knowing that consciousness expresses itself as form and non-form. Right action is a Buddhist concept described as a spontaneous, unconditioned, and intuitional insight enabling one to respond appropriately to what appears and disappears in our awareness.

Right action is not about judging our actions as good or bad but rather about responding to the present moment appropriately without being subjected to unreal assumptions or expectations. The now-moment is not a series of conceptual ideas. It is experienced spontaneously by what appears and disappears in our awareness and through our sense perceptions. Without the coloration of conceptual thought, one is freed from preconceived reactions. The correct action occurs spontaneously. It opens intuitive experiences that clarify what is being experienced.

With the cessation of conceptual thinking, there are no preferences or a predetermined reality that the mind fabricates through an intellectual process. This makes it possible to choose (in the present moment) what is appropriate at the time. This can be expressed as a preference when it is in accordance and aligned with the experience. When you are free, you can see what the right thing to do is! Right action becomes spontaneous and appropriate when one's actions are aligned with the demands of the present moment. Our actions are expressed in an awakened consciousness that is free to be the unconditional intelligence of the "now-moment." You are the now-moment that is manifesting your life. You can experience this existence "as it is" without judgment or commentary.

Chapter 23

The Universal Mind and the Wisdom Mind

The Universal Mind

Many say that the Universal mind is the mind of God. It is universal because it exists beyond the human mind's conditioning. It functions through a universal perception that sees the wholeness of all that exists and perceives the reality of the universe's creative and destructive forces. It is an awareness that sees the big picture and is not confined to attachments or limitations. And it doesn't have a personal identity as humans do. The universal mind is connected to everything individually and collectively.

When one's human mind is tapped into the Universal mind, there's no dualistic relationship, and it is not separated into divisions or categories. The Universal mind has unlimited resources fundamental to its being the primordial consciousness of all. Its connection to everything is expressed as the unified fabric of pure consciousness manifested as existence. This connection is universal!

The Wisdom Mind

The "wisdom mind" is an intuitive mind. Its wisdom comes from a universal intelligence that provides mental insight not contrived by conceptual thought. It thrives as an intuitive wisdom of knowing that is spontaneous and effortless and can only be experienced in the present moment. Its wisdom goes beyond a conceptual mind and knows the appropriate action for every interaction. Its presence is in the silence of the present moment without a past or future.

The wisdom mind transcends ordinary thinking and connects with a deeper, intuitive understanding of reality. It involves accessing higher levels of awareness and insight. The wisdom mind is associated with cultivating not just a state of being but a transformative force that inspires change. It is wisdom derived through insightful practices such as meditation and self-realization. It consists of gaining insight into reality's true nature and overcoming ignorance and illusion. The wisdom mind is the mind of a self-realized being. It is connected to the Universal Mind and functions as the authentic and higher self in the enlightened being. It is integrated with their intellect, functioning together as one.

The Wisdom-mind can be hidden or veiled by conceptual thought. It can be so hidden that it never occurs to the seeker that they're trapped inside a bubble of conceptual untruths. The wisdom mind is unveiled as the ego is revealed and surrendered. This is the culmination of truth that prevails with enlightenment.

Chapter 24: Guru Nitya Chaitanya Yati

Chapter 24

Guru Nitya Chaitanya Yati

The Guru: What and Who is a Guru?

In the Sanskrit language, the word "Guru" (गुरु) is defined as:

- "Gu" (गु): meaning "darkness, ignorance, heaviness"
- "Ru" (रु): meaning "remover, dispeller, light"

Therefore, literally, "Guru" translates to "one who dispels darkness" or "one who removes ignorance."

This etymology reflects the more profound role of a Guru in Indian traditions. They are not just teachers:

- They help spiritual seekers to overcome the darkness of ignorance and illusion, leading them toward spiritual enlightenment.

- They share their wisdom and understanding of the Divine, illuminating the path for their seekers.

- They embody the qualities and practices they teach, providing a living example for their followers.

Overall, the Sanskrit definition of "Guru" paints a powerful image of a guide who enlightens, uplifts, and empowers seekers on their spiritual journeys.

Guru Nitya and My Relationship with the Guru

Guru Nitya Chaitanya Yati: His name in Sanskrit means "(Nitya) Eternal (Chaitanya) Pure Consciousness," and Yati means one who has control over his desires and attachments.

Guru Nitya, as his followers call him, is from South India. His notable spiritual path is Vedanta, particularly Advaita Vedanta. He is brilliantly intellectual, well-read, and educated, with a wealth of knowledge in psychology, philosophy, and metaphysics.

For me, it was sometimes intimidating to be with him. Between his intellectual and intuitive abilities, I felt he could see right through me, knowing what my mind was thinking. Sometimes, when I was confused, I asked the Guru to clarify my position.. He might be silent for a day or two. Then, he would say something while interacting with a group or conversing with someone, which would trigger an insight that I knew he was talking directly to me. He would say precisely the answer or insight I needed at the right time.

Another side of the dynamic relationship between a Guru and his students is uplifting them out of their darkness and negative past. Most people harbor a dark side or shadow that is negative in content, hidden from conscious awareness, and often harmful to a person's well-being. If you turn the light on these shadows and confront them, they are exposed and can be dealt with or eliminated. This happens in the Guru's presence; the light dispels the darkness.

Meeting the Guru

I met "Guru Nitya," as his followers call him, in San Francisco in 1974. I saw him at the Sivananda Center, where I attended a yoga event. He didn't speak at this event but was there more as a spiritual presence to support the event. I was drawn to his silence and composure. He seemed to be in meditation throughout the event. Afterward, I asked a person who appeared to be one of his followers if I could meet him. They said to come to where he was staying and that he would meet me there.

So, after the event, I went to where he was staying and entered the house, where a woman greeted me. I asked if I could meet with the Guru and was told to sit down and make the request mentally in my mind, and he would come down from his room to meet me. I followed her instructions, and after 5 or 10 minutes, he came down and asked if I wanted to talk to him.

We went to the kitchen and sat down at the kitchen table. I asked him if he was my Guru. He said, "No, I am not your Guru". He was very polite and had a peaceful, silent presence that was pervasive and almost hypnotic. We briefly talked, and I was somewhat stunned by his responses.

Several days later, I was told that he was speaking at a yoga event and that I might want to attend. I went to the event and sat in the back of the room. My mind was turned inward, and I was meditative, which made me seem to connect to his silence. In my mind, I asked if he would be my Guru. This was a heartfelt request.

Initiation

After a few days of meeting Guru Nitya, my friend and yoga teacher called to say he wanted to meet me. I was anxious about meeting him again. We met at a friend's house, and he agreed to initiate me on his spiritual path. I've journeyed on this path without disrupting our relationship since then.

When I first met Nitya, I didn't understand what he meant when he told me he was not my Guru. It wasn't until several years later that I had the opportunity to be with him again when he visited me in Florida. Here, we had many silent interactions and private times where I could assimilate his vibrations and insights from his presence and teachings.

At the end of the visit, he told me I would never see him again. He said that I shouldn't be attached to his physical appearance in my life. He told me that the true Guru is my authentic self, the same as the Guru's self. There isn't any difference. And that this relationship has always been present as Eternal Pure Consciousness. The same consciousness that takes all forms.

My Experience with Guru Nitya

A few weeks after being with "Nitya" (as his followers call him), he left for Portland, OR, and I had to stay behind to work. The night he left, I had a sudden feeling of darkness and depression that, out of nowhere, appeared in my mind. At the time, I didn't know how this came about or why.

I eventually learned that it was what's called "The Dark Night of the Soul." I now believe that the Guru's light illuminated the unreal aspects of my mind and opened a Pandora's box. Here, it was revealed that I was the fabricated person I assumed to be myself. Everything I thought I was accomplishing, my lifestyle, the possessions I had acquired, and the friendships I valued suddenly appeared as a bad dream. All of this and all the memories of my life's experiences had no value whatsoever. I felt this was the darkest place I'd ever experienced. I saw how wrongful identities appeared authentic, and these illusions had destructive emotions attached. This was a very depressing experience.

The Guru's light illuminates and destroys all that is not true. There's a prominent thought that the seeker may not be capable of resisting the Guru's "white heat" if they stay in his presence for a long time. Even temporarily, one may not survive getting burnt up by the Guru's light.

The ego is threatened by an experience such as the Dark Night of the Soul. So much of the subconscious programming gets exposed by the Guru, and the Guru reveals himself over and over again to be your highest self, as well. There's only a unified consciousness that takes on different appearances, and its energy is like the ocean waves that appear in various shapes and qualities. The waves and the ocean never become separated because they are always one. This is the same as the Guru's relationship to his students. It's not a devotion to a man.

Transmission of Truth

The Gurus' physical appearance should be distinct from the Guru. The experience of the Guru and student is a transmission of wisdom and knowledge that reveals a presence of the vibrant truth beyond the boundaries of body and mind, dualistic thinking, or light and darkness. "That" which is beyond this or that. I am That! You are That! We are That! Singular and without concepts, ideas, attachments, preferences, biased opinions, false identities, and even beyond a neutral experience of understanding.

The light of the Guru's presence is a burning light that extinguishes anything that is not real. Being in proximity to this burning light can cause the demise of the ego. The ego doesn't exist in reality and is false! Therefore, the burning fire of Guru's presence exposes and dispels all false narratives and fabrications conditioned by the mind.

The Path of Advaita Vedanta

"Vedanta" is a compound word formed by joining two parts:

- "Veda" (वेद) means "knowledge, wisdom, scripture."
- "anta" (अन्त) means "end, goal, conclusion."

Therefore, the most literal translation of "Vedanta" is "the end of the Vedas"(Scriptures) or "the conclusion of knowledge." This is most suited for realizing the self as the conclusion of disassociating with conceptual thinking and transcending the mind. In other words, there's nothing else to search for.

In a broader sense, "Vedanta" can signify the pursuit of ultimate knowledge and liberation from misidentification and attachments. It represents the quest for understanding the true nature of reality, the connection between individual and universal consciousness, and the ultimate goal of human existence. The emphasis lies in seeking wisdom and liberation through meditation, contemplation, self-realization, and knowing the ultimate Reality (Brahman or God). This has been my path for over 40 years.

VERBAL & NON-VERBAL REALITY

The path of Advaita Vedanta means "nondual" in Sanskrit. It aims to help you realize your true nature as Brahman or God, the "one" nondual reality underlying all existence. It's a journey of understanding yourself not as a separate individual soul but as identical to universal consciousness. A qualified spiritual Guru can guide you in understanding and applying these experiences and practices.

Conclusion

What I have shared and discussed in this book is my personal experience and how I view what is real and what is not. It has been my life's commitment and spiritual journey to traverse this phenomenal existence as a human being. I have shared my thoughts and experience of what I call a conceptual realization. This led me to search for decades and inspired me to share my views. In this exploration, I have delved deeply into the mechanics of the mind in many ways that have fulfilled all I sought. I am no longer searching for anything. This journey opened the door to an insightful understanding of my purpose and commitment to an enlightened intent that took more than 60 years. I hope anyone who reads this will understand their true nature and become aware of the conceptual realities they experience in this verbal reality. I've shared these insights with you and hope they will be as valuable to you as you traverse your life's journey. I'm not saying that the journey ends. Every moment is committed to realizing and contemplating what is phenomenal and what is Absolute. A spiritual awareness of what has been discovered is a neverending realization from moment to moment.

Verbal reality is such an essential aspect of the human condition. It touches every aspect of our lives and is necessary for us to interact intellectually and understand each other. This is what distinguishes us as human beings from other animals. However, as digital language matrices are artificial, so is the language matrix of human thought and emotion. Even though its importance is essential for transactional and interactional experiences, we should consider its impact on our lives and how limited and contracted our awareness and consciousness can be.

In Part I, I explored how a conceptual matrix creates a verbal reality that most people are conditioned to experience without conscious awareness. I hope you have understood the illusive mind and benefited from this discourse.

In Part II, we examined some aspects of nonverbal reality. A spiritual journey to self-realization is illuminated by understanding the elements and practices of silence, presence, and metaphysical awareness, all revealing "what is" when all appearances are perceived "as they are." This journey into realizing the Self becomes effortless once you know its ever-present existence as a silent presence that underlies all phenomena. Nonconceptual wisdom is experienced in silence, known as "silent being," providing a cohesive and insightful understanding of what is not real. I hope that, in some way, you see that consciousness and awareness are your true Self.

We are entering a new age of information and technological advancement that will either enlighten or destroy humanity as we know it. The Age of Aquarius is the new age of enlightenment, where the light of knowledge dawns on the earth's inhabitants. As humanity enters a new phase of awareness and enlightenment, it will transform the human race and enlighten all to know their "true being."

I hope this book has raised each reader's awareness to a higher level so that they can be aware and experience themselves as they are without bias or judgment. This would begin the collective elimination of all that is untrue and unreal in our societies. You are blessed, and I hope this book has opened your mind to see all appearances as they are and to know what is real and what is not.

About the Author

Mike Marinelli

The author has been on a journey of inquiry and discovery into what, why, and how existence came into being and how it has sustained its appearance for over eight decades.

His spiritual journey began in early childhood in the Southern Baptist tradition in London Bridge, Virginia. In 1964, he began practicing Zen Meditation, which was spiritually inspired by Alan Watts. In 1968, he began attending Zen meditation at the Los Angeles Zen Center. In 1972, he moved to San Francisco and began practicing Raja Yoga (controlling thought content in the mind). He met his Guru in 1974 in San Francisco, CA.

In this three-dimensional experience of reality, the author's journey has explored topics such as linguistics, awareness, consciousness, meditation, self-realization, and metaphysics.

He's a lifetime spiritual practitioner and musician. He's an instrumentalist, playing clarinets, saxophones, electronic wind instruments, and Native American Flutes. He began studying music in public school at age 9. In his spiritual journey, he never retreated from an ordinary life's entanglements, and his insights came from his participation and interactions in his work-related and spiritual experiences. Awareness was always the key to unlocking the mysteries of his spiritual journey, and he abides in this awareness as his true self.

Throughout his music career, he worked at many "day gigs" to support his family. He was a musician, occupational therapist, financial planner, real estate agent, Information Technology support technician, retail sales representative, janitorial entrepreneur, and music teacher. These positions provided him with multiple occupational vocabularies and conceptual realities, which helped him understand these topics. Empirical knowledge provided the information and insights he has shared with the reader.

Appendix I

The Guru's perspective and insights are helpful in understanding the awakening to what is untrue and what has been conditioned by fabrications of reality. This excerpt presents a comprehensive understanding of my Guru's visions and insights in this discourse.

Psychology of Darsanamala

Commentary by Guru Nitya Chaitanya Yati: Chapter VIII, verse 4

Atma (true Self) alone is Brahman (God)

The knower of the Self (the Absolute Self) contemplates the Atma, not any other

This thus meditating the Self is named as Bhakti (Devotional Contemplation)

Guru's Commentary

If ignorance is like an ocean of darkness, knowledge is like an island of light where rises the resplendent sun of pure consciousness. Although darkness is negative, it does have the capacity to conceal truth and obstruct vision. When light comes, it does not push away darkness. The very presence of light is the absence of darkness. Light not only causes its own existence but it also automatically reveals its presence. It not only presents itself but also illuminates whatever is within its ambit.

The light that is spoken of here is not physical light but the illuminating and self-revealing qualities of consciousness. The self-revealing consciousness is the *Atma* or *the existent self.* The revelation is not to any agent other than the Self because nothing else exists except the negativity of non-knowledge.

Although effort is required for a person to free himself of the ten thousand and one colorations and conditionings that come to his mind, once he is free of the tyranny of inhibitory or obsessive compulsions, consciousness effortlessly shines forth without having any need to dismiss the unreal. And although there can be a relativisitic increase or decrease of physical light, or in the cognitive clarity of apprehending and discerning objects of perceptual or conceptual import, there exist no such degrees of comparison in consciousness that is pure, simple, and homogeneous. This is not a state that is manifesting, but it is what truly is and what is veiled by the phenomenon of relativism, which is comparable to the kaleidoscopic tapestry of mental images. In the conditioned state, innumerable are the objects for the mind to meditate on, but in the uncondiioned state the Self alone is, and it has not a second to be with. Hence, we can say it has become the all-filling Brahma (God) which is never again tampered with by the advent of anything conditional, eventual, or consequential. This pure state is called Bhakti. In this spiritual flight a person has two aids. One is called *guru* and the other is called *bhakti.* Guru means "The dispeller of darkness." Bhakti means "conjunction with light."

(D.K. Printworld (P) Ltd. Reprinted edition 2004, 2017: Bhakti Darshana, Chapter VIII, verse 4, p. 376 - 378 Narayana Gurukala)

Appendix II

Birth and Death: Are they real?

One's allegiance to a fabricated reality, unsubstantiated by the truth of the Absolute, has positioned us to experience an unreality caused by a linguistic matrix that is a conceptualized fabrication of what is real. Attachments to conditioned conceptualization have imprisoned our minds to succumb to unreal values, beliefs, and misinformation.

Among these untruths is the belief that our body and mind exist as a person. This relativistic truth is imagined and conceived only through conceptualization. The idea of birth and death are extreme concepts that conceptualization identifies as truth. It is not true when the conceptualized reality is abolished.

As I see it, the remedy exposes this untruth through meditation, contemplation, and self-inquiry, as understood and realized by many enlightened beings. The path of non-duality is explicit. Without a conceptual reality and the thinking mind, one is relieved of a fabricated phenomenon we believe is real. Instead of subjects and objects coming and going in our awareness, we become aware of an empty awareness that is pure consciousness beyond these dualities.

So, the concepts of birth and death are unsubstantiated once these concepts are transcended and the waves of individuality are absorbed back into the ocean of the Absolute. The self-realization is that the only thing substantiated is the Absolute, which the mind or the ego cannot comprehend because it is beyond conceptual fabrication. Birth and death never existed! These ideas are purely conceptual.

Here, we enter the realm of the unknown. I only know who I am if I conceptualize an answer. I need conceptualization to know who I am, and if I "think" I know, I can only know this as a fabricated person created by language and the conceptual mind. Who is it that knows who they are? Who is the thinker of these thoughts and concepts? The silent presence of being cannot be comprehended or verbally expressed without answering these questions with language and thoughts. So, what exists? When all conceptual thinking is abolished, the ego and its identifications vanish effortlessly.

An imaginative mind and collective conditioning fabricated all ideas of birth, death, and such dualities. Can anyone attain the state of Nirvana or Samadhi? It can't happen! Who is going to experience it? The conceptually fabricated and unsubstantiated ego? It is only possible to understand this or anything related to it if we conceptualize it, proving that birth and death are untruths and have been a fabrication of a conceptualized reality.